BRUCE LEE'S
5 METHODS OF

SAMMY FRANCO

Also by Sammy Franco

The Heavy Bag Bible
The Widow Maker Compendium
Invincible: Mental Toughness Techniques for Peak Performance
Unleash Hell: A Step-by-Step Guide to Devastating Widow Maker Combinations
Feral Fighting: Advanced Widow Maker Fighting Techniques
The Widow Maker Program: Extreme Self-Defense for Deadly Force Situations
Savage Street Fighting: Tactical Savagery as a Last Resort
Heavy Bag Workout
Heavy Bag Combinations
Heavy Bag Training
The Complete Body Opponent Bag Book
Stand and Deliver: A Street Warrior's Guide to Tactical Combat Stances
Maximum Damage: Hidden Secrets Behind Brutal Fighting Combinations
First Strike: End a Fight in Ten Seconds or Less!
The Bigger They Are, The Harder They Fall
Self-Defense Tips and Tricks
Kubotan Power: Quick & Simple Steps to Mastering the Kubotan Keychain
Gun Safety: For Home Defense and Concealed Carry
Out of the Cage: A Guide to Beating a Mixed Martial Artist on the Street
Warrior Wisdom: Inspiring Ideas from the World's Greatest Warriors
War Machine: How to Transform Yourself Into a Vicious and Deadly Street Fighter
1001 Street Fighting Secrets
When Seconds Count: Self-Defense for the Real World
Killer Instinct: Unarmed Combat for Street Survival
Street Lethal: Unarmed Urban Combat

Bruce Lee's 5 Methods of Attack
Copyright © 2015 by Sammy Franco
ISBN: 978-1-941845-23-3
Printed in the United States of America

Published by Contemporary Fighting Arts, LLC.
Visit us Online at: **SammyFranco.com**

For author interviews or publicity information, please send inquiries in care of the publisher.

Contents

"Absorb what is useful, reject what is useless, add what is specifically your own."

– Bruce Lee

Warning!

The self-defense techniques, tactics, methods, and information described and depicted in this book can be dangerous and could result in serious injury and or death and should not be used or practiced in any way without the guidance of a professional reality based self-defense instructor.

The author, publisher, and distributors of this book disclaim any liability from loss, injury, or damage, personal or otherwise, resulting from the information and procedures in this book. *This book is for academic study only.*

Before you begin any exercise program, including those suggested in this book, it is important to check with your physician to see if you have any condition that might be aggravated by strenuous exercise.

About This Book!

Very few people can argue that Bruce Lee was one of the greatest martial artists of all time. Besides being a Hollywood action star, Lee was also a devoted husband and father, athlete, philosopher, writer and teacher.

Most people, however, don't realize that Bruce Lee was also a brilliant martial arts innovator who dedicated his life in search of self-knowledge and personal expression. Armed with a library of more than 2,000 books, Lee arduously and painstakingly gathered, analyzed, tested, and documented information relevant to his quest for martial truth.

For over nineteen years, Bruce conducted both academic and practical research. Luckily, he documented and recorded his ideas and discoveries. It wasn't until after his shocking and untimely death that his lifelong research was published in his book, Tao of Jeet Kune Do.

One of Bruce Lee's most notable discoveries was his Five Ways of Attack. These methodologies include:

- **Attack by Drawing (ABD)**
- **Hand Immobilization Attack (HIA)**
- **Progressive Indirect Attack (PIA)**
- **Simple Direct Attack (SDA) & Single Angular Attack (SAA)**
- **Attack By Combination (ABC)**

These five methods of attack were Lee's personal road map for fighting success. Unfortunately, for most people, these unique fighting techniques are difficult to understand and almost impossible to apply.

Therefore, the goal of this book is twofold. First, it gives you a rare glimpse into the world of martial arts innovation that few people ever know. This in turn will provide you with a greater understanding and appreciation of Lee's work.

Second, it analyzes Bruce Lee's fighting methods and breaks them down into simple, no-nonsense concepts and strategies that anyone can understand and apply. Here you'll find, clear and concise instructions and detailed photographs for implementing Bruce Lee's devastating and legendary fighting methods under real-world combat conditions.

In this book, you'll also discover that not all of Lee's methods of attack are suitable for the average person. Recognizing and understanding the limitations in some of the fighting methods could mean the difference between victory and defeat. In a high-risk self-defense situation, this could mean the difference between life and death.

- *Sammy Franco*

Bruce Lee and his son Brandon 1966.

Chapter One
Innovation In The Martial Arts

Prerequisites to Martial Arts Innovation

Before discussing the specific methods of attack, it's important that you have a solid understanding of martial arts innovation. Only then can you truly appreciate the totality of Bruce Lee's work.

I hope to give the readers of this book a closer look into my own search and accomplishment at martial arts innovation. First, I will provide an intellectual overview of the foundation, premise, and research necessary for valid innovation. Second, I will provide a glimpse of the sacrifices and emotional struggle necessary for such efforts.

Innovation in the martial arts is not a modern phenomenon. Contrary to popular misconception, innovation did not begin and end with Bruce Lee. Although Lee was one of our foremost contemporary innovators, innovation is as old as the martial arts themselves. In fact, many of the traditional martial arts are the product of innovation. The annals are full of examples: Jigoro Kano (Judo), Morihei Ueshiba (Aikido), and Kokaku Takeda (Daito Ryu) are but a few.

Although martial innovation is not new, there is a troublesome trend developing among many of today's practitioners. It is the tendency to launch cavalierly off to proclaim new systems of self-defense, supposedly each one better than the last. In fact, far too many of these so-called innovators are motivated for all the wrong reasons. Some seek ego gratification, money, or fame, while others simply lack the discipline to persevere in a particular martial art.

Many practitioners are unaware of the inherent complexity, responsibility, and sacrifice of valid innovation. They fail to realize that innovation is an evolutionary process of modification and refinement, rather than a revolutionary product rendered out of whole cloth. It takes serious intellectual analysis and research, not to mention strategic experimentation. Motivation must come from deep within the soul, heart, and mind. The search for martial truth must become an obsession.

Morihei Ueshiba, the founder of Aikido.

The Foundation

It's absurd to think of founding a new method of self-defense without an extensive foundation in the martial arts and related disciplines. By foundation, I am not referring to superficial excursions into various systems or sciences. A knowledgeable foundation can be built only on consistent training and extensive study. All great innovators were obsessed with training and study, and each had an extensive foundation in the sciences before even considering innovation.

A strong foundation establishes the physical, mental, and spiritual attributes of the true martial scientist. Extensive physical training develops and refines the physical attributes of self-defense (i.e., speed, power, timing, balance, accuracy, fluidity, etc.). A broad intellectual grasp of various combat sciences and strategic concepts is critical to any effort to modify and refine. Theoretical and conceptual analyses are touchstones of innovation. Finally, a sound foundation will begin to open the practitioner's inner self to the spiritual component of the martial arts. An innovator must become his art.

Simply put, there are no shortcuts! Every innovator starts at the bottom and works his or her way up. The greatest were beginners (white belts, if you will). If you are unprepared to embrace the rudiments, forget rushing ahead to modify or create. A martial arts innovator can only succeed with a deep comprehension of the various tools, techniques, and related elements of the arts. Innovation requires that you learn to walk before you run.

The Premise

Innovation in every major field is based on a premise. The premise may be an axiom, a concept, a rule, or any other valid reason to modify or go beyond that which has already been established. Generally speaking, a valid premise is the consummation of an analytical process. It is not something simply "thought up" or created on whim or fancy.

Every foundational premise for innovation has roots in what has gone before. For example, in science Einstein's theory of relativity would not have come about without Newtonian physics and the significant prior discoveries in electromagnetic physics. In art, the cubists and abstract expressionists owed much to the discoveries of traditional realists.

The same is true for the martial sciences. Modifications and innovations in the sciences are based upon scientifically established premises. Premises for martial innovation may be the result of cultural eccentricities, moral codes, or any number of other factors, including geography and topography. For example, historians attribute the development of acrobatic high kicks of northern kung-fu styles to the tall grassy plains upon which combat was waged. In contrast, the rapid hand movements and lower stances of some southern styles are attributed to the urban terrain.

Given the critical role of the premise for innovation, it is disturbing that far too many modern "innovators" set out to create and promote new styles or systems without the background, study, and analysis necessary to formulate a valid reason for change. I know for a fact that some of these self-proclaimed vanguards are motivated for all the wrong reasons.

For example, the innovator would not discard a high-line kick because the former takes too much time, flexibility, and coordination to master. He may establish legitimate reasons for advocating the low-line kick over the dramatic high-line kick, but only after mastering both and then articulating very specific strategic premises and conditions for using one over the other.

In my case, I have devoted more than a decade to training, studying, researching, and analyzing the martial arts. This eventually led me to the awareness that many essential concepts, methods, and tactics were not being taught or established in American martial art schools. More and more it became alarmingly obvious to me that too much information was being neglected. My primary concern centered on the aggressive and destructive capacity of the hard-core street criminal. Consequently, the premise of my Contemporary

Fighting Arts (CFA) system was formulated on efficiency, effectiveness, and safety geared entirely to real life self-defense situations.

The Research

Research is a continuous and painstaking process of gathering, analyzing, testing, and documenting information relevant to the innovator's premise. There are two broad categories of research that, in reality, overlap in very significant ways: academic and practical research.

Academic research is a scholarly process requiring dedication, patience, and an insatiable desire to learn. The innovator truly must want to know all there is! Once again, his premise enters the picture in the all-important role of a beacon, directing him to information that has some relevance and bearing on his ultimate goal. Without this direction he is likely to waste time sorting and separating valuable data from a tremendous amount of junk.

Academic research involves voracious reading. The body of printed materials on martial arts and self-defense has grown astronomically over the last 40 years. Moreover, martial art instructional videos have added a whole new and interesting database, and provocative seminars are offered around the country. But let me offer a word of caution: the innovator can't just expose himself passively to these sources. Literature must be dissected and noted. Videos must be viewed over and over again.

Strategically sound and weak points should be recorded and analyzed in personal journals. And finally, seminars and training programs should be attended with an open mind, balanced with healthy skepticism.

Practical research thus begins. The innovator's information has been analyzed, cross-referenced, and refined to theoretical applications. It's time to back away from the blackboard and head for the lab.

Obviously there are some difficulties in approaching safe and sound practical or experimental research. One of the axioms of CFA is that experimentation in the face of danger is an invitation to disaster. The last place in the world the innovator wants to test his theories is in a real encounter. Somehow, somewhere, he has got to get it right before the real thing happens.

The training academy is the answer, but it is a troublesome one. The innovator will need loyal, trustworthy, and tough colleagues to test the results of his findings. Perfecting tools, techniques, and strategies takes a lot of time and most likely will result in injuries. There simply is no way to test the innovator's hypotheses without the situational reality they've been designed to address. In common parlance, the innovator can't pull punches. Otherwise, he risks dangerous uncertainty. On the other hand, an innovator should never conduct practical research on students. His theories must be refined only with those he can trust, who share his vision.

Finally, once the innovator's academic and practical research have been compatibly merged and his hypothesis adequately tested, he will be in a position to crystallize and articulate a martial truth. Over time this process and the resulting truths will build. Eventually, if successful, the innovator's research will lead to the structuring of a complex array of combative truths. This will be the innovator's system, the culmination of innovation.

Profile of the Innovator

The personalities of martial innovators differ greatly. Some have been eccentric and curious characters. Others are very mainstream and seemingly ordinary people. Across of this broad-spectrum, however, are certain common qualities and characteristics.

Perhaps the most commonly shared characteristics among real martial innovators is a deep and enduring love of the martial arts. The world is experienced and analyzed through a unique filter separating out everything that has no relevance or bearing on their vision and search for martial truth. To most people, this unique group of martial scientists are likely to appear singularly obsessed, perhaps fanatical, in their immersion in the arts.

A martial innovators lifestyle is reflective of the martial way. He maintains excellent physical conditioning. Destructive habits are shunned. Excessive consumption, drugs and other forms of decadence are evils to be avoided. Corruption, greed and immorality are rejected in favor of society's laws, morals and ethical codes.

Self-confidence is imperative. The innovator will find himself under intense scrutiny and criticism which can lead to an overwhelming sense of alienation. To retain his courage and vision, the innovator must resort ultimately to self-trust and confidence.

Psychological and emotional maturity plays a big role, not age. This is a wellspring of strength and fortitude to cope with the pitfalls and pressures of this unique lifestyle. This maturity also provides the insight and wisdom necessary to defeat self-delusion and harmful ego gratification.

To launch out on a mission of innovation and refinement requires great heart and courage. But it also takes spiritual strength, wisdom, and maturity. Practitioners who have succeeded in attaining the visions of truth have been blessed with a unique blend of these complex characteristics and traits.

The Pitfalls of Innovation

No matter how skillful you are or the extent of your intellectual and technical knowledge, the hardships and sacrifices will challenge your very being.

Chapter One: Innovation In The Martial Arts

An innovator who wishes to make a meaningful contribution to the martial arts must be prepared to dedicate his life to the discipline. Even then, there is no guarantee he will reach the mountaintop.

Time, time and more time. You'll spend years learning a particular style, system or methodology, perfecting the most basic physical maneuvers, and developing a strong foundation. For most people, the time it takes to reach this level of accomplishment is all they can afford. For the innovator, these years represent only the beginning of their journey.

Slowly - ever so slowly - the doors of understanding and insight open. A faint vision appears in the artist's mind's eye. Experimentation and research begin. The vision is refined. But this process is too time-consuming, so painstakingly slow, and at first it is perceived as a series of tiny steps on an endless path.

Innovation is like building a stone wall. But before the wall goes up you have to travel to another continent to gather the stones, carry them home, and then carve and shape them to fit accurately one with the other. The frustration and confusion are tremendous. You will run full speed down dead end alleys, and trip blindfolded into dangerous ravines.

You will develop, shape and articulate a concept or principle as truth, only to be later rejected as folly. I am reminded of the great Austrian philosopher Ludwig Wittgenstein, who precipitously and radically rejected his entire theory on logical analysis in favor of a new vision now accepted as modern truth in linguistic analysis. Fortunately, my own reversals have not been this radical but I've been forced to continuously review and refine my own system. For example, at one time I advocated the use of feints in street combat. Through further research, I later rejected this technique.

In conjunction with the time-consuming process of

experimentation, research and refinement, you must devote substantial time to keeping your physical skills tuned up, reading everything you can get your hands on, possibly teaching, and trying to balance the other aspects of your life. In no time at all your spouse, your family and friends let you know that you are neglecting other commitments. So you steal a little time from your passion to patch up other demands. It is an endless give and take which regrettably does not always work.

On top of all this, unless you're independently wealthy, learn to love poverty. No one is going to pay you to pursue your vision of martial truth. And there simply is not enough time to achieve honest accomplishment in innovation and pursue an unrelated career too. The answer is a part-time job that allows you to make ends meet (sort of) but more importantly allows ample free time for the arts. Be prepared to accept financial hardships while your peers and colleagues remind you of the promotions advancements they are making in nice paying regular jobs.

In the end, be prepared to be alone, financially stopped, and subject to substantial criticism and complaint. You'll have your share of sleepless nights filled with doubts regarding your personal life and your martial vision.

Finally, be prepared to have your system rejected by the martial arts community. Venerable masters are skeptical of anyone claiming to have refined or created something other than that which has existed for hundreds of years. But this skepticism is healthy. It functions as a filtering system which rids us of charlatans and tests the theories and hypotheses of innovators. At the same time, skepticism must remain balanced to avoid cynicism, close-mindedness, and bias. The innovator should expect his vision to be tested by other legitimate skeptics and closed-minded cynics. Even when his truth has been adequately expressed to the former, he will not necessarily receive warm and ready recognition. Once again, be prepared to stand your ground comforted only by the self-satisfaction of having expressed and attained your vision of truth. For the real martial arts innovator, this will be reward enough.

Bruce Lee's 5 Methods of Attack

Chapter Two
Fighting Tools and Techniques

Things You'll Need to Know!

In order to appreciate and apply the various methods of attack discussed in the next chapter, it's important to have a grasp of the following elements of unarmed combat. They are:

- **Ranges of Combat**
- **The Fighting Stance**
- **Footwork and Mobility**
- **Combat Attributes**
- **Tools and Techniques**
- **Anatomical Targets**

The Ranges of Unarmed Combat

Real wold fighting is unpredictable. It can happen anytime and anywhere. If you want to be prepared to handle any type of attack, you'd better be range proficient. Range proficiency is the skill and ability to fight your adversary in all three distances of unarmed combat (kicking range, punching range, and grappling range).

This means that you are capable of fighting an opponent in all possible situations. For example, can you fight an assailant on a bus, in a crowded bar? While lying in your bed or sitting in your car? Do you have the skill to strike an assailant standing five feet away from you? These and other questions pertain to range proficiency.

In unarmed combat, there are only three possible distances from which you can engage your opponent: kicking range, punching range, and grappling range. However, for the purposes of this book, I will also be addressing a fourth distance called trapping range. Let's begin with the kicking range.

Kicking Range

At this distance, you are usually too far to make contact with your hands, so you would use your legs to strike your assailant. For self-defense, you should only employ low-line kicks. These are directed to targets below the assailant's waist, such as the groin, thigh, knee joint, and shin. As a result, I teach my students to use kicking range tools like the vertical, push, side, and hook kicks. They are safe, efficient, and destructive.

The kicking distance of unarmed combat.

Punching Range

This is the midrange of unarmed combat. At this distance, you are close enough to the opponent to strike him with your hands. Hand strikes do not require as much room as kicking, and the surface area that you are standing on is not as crucial a concern.

Effective punching range techniques include the following:: finger jabs, palm heels, knife hands, lead straights, rear crosses, horizontal and shovel hooks, uppercuts, and hammer fists.

The punching range of unarmed combat.

Grappling Range

The third and closest range of unarmed combat is grappling range. At this distance, you are too close to your opponent to kick or execute some hand strikes, so you would use close-quarter tools and techniques to neutralize your adversary.

Grappling range is divided into two different planes: vertical and horizontal. In the vertical plane, you would deliver impact techniques, some of which include elbow and knee strikes, head butts, gouging and crushing tactics, and biting and tearing techniques.

In the horizontal plane, you are ground fighting with your enemy and can deliver all of the

The grappling range (vertical plane).

previously mentioned techniques, including various submission holds, locks, and chokes.

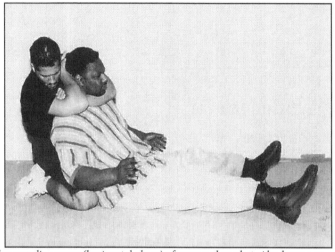

The grappling range (horizontal plane) of unarmed combat. Also known as ground fighting.

Trapping Range

Trapping range is the distance between punching and grappling range and it's used by practitioners who are skilled in the art of hand immobilization (trapping). At this proximity the practitioner can use

The trapping range.

a variety of highly complex moves and counter moves to control the opponent's limbs and prevent him from executing an offense attack. Trapping techniques may be applied against arms and hands or legs. Generally, however, the more intricate trapping techniques involve the upper gates, i.e., the arms and hands. For more information see, Hand Immobilization Attack (HIA) in the next chapter.

The Fighting Stance

The fighting stance defines your ability to execute both offensive and defensive techniques, and it will play a material role in the outcome of a combat situation. It stresses strategic soundness and simplicity over complexity and style. The fighting stance also facilitates optimum execution of your body weapons while simultaneously protecting your vital targets against quick counter strikes.

The fighting stance is designed around the centerline. The centerline is an imaginary vertical line running through the center of the body, from the top of your head to the bottom of the groin. Most of your vital targets are situated along this line, including the head, throat, solar plexus, and groin. Obviously, you want to avoid directly exposing your centerline to the assailant. To achieve this, position your feet and body at a 45-degree angle from the opponent. This moves your body targets back and away from direct strikes but leaves you strategically positioned to attack.

When assuming a fighting stance, place your

The centerline.

strongest and most coordinated side forward. For example, a right-handed person stands with his or her right side toward the assailant. Keeping your strongest side forward enhances the speed, power, and accuracy of your lead strike. This doesn't mean that you should never practice fighting from your other side. You must be capable of fighting from both sides, and you should spend equal practice time on the left and right stances.

The right lead fighting stance.   *The Left lead fighting stance.*

Don't make the costly mistake of stepping forward to assume a fighting stance. This action only moves you closer to your assailant before your protective structure is soundly established. Moving closer to your assailant also dramatically reduces your defensive reaction time. So get into the habit of stepping backward to assume your stance. Practice this daily until it becomes a natural movement.

How to Assume a Fighting Stance

When assuming your fighting stance, place your feet about shoulder width apart. Keep your knees bent and flexible. Think of your legs as power springs to launch you through the ranges of unarmed combat (kicking, punching, and grappling range).

Mobility is also important, as we'll discuss later. All footwork and strategic movement should be performed on the balls of your feet. Your weight distribution is also an important factor. Since combat is dynamic, your weight distribution will frequently change. However, when stationary, keep 50 percent of your body weight on each leg and always be in control of it.

The hands are aligned one behind the other along your centerline. The lead arm is held high and bent at approximately 90 degrees. The rear arm is kept back by the chin. Arranged this way, the hands not only protect the upper centerline but also allow quick deployment of your body weapons. When holding your guard, do not tighten your shoulder or arm muscles prior to striking. Stay relaxed and loose. Finally, keep your chin slightly angled down. This diminishes target size and reduces the likelihood of a paralyzing blow to your chin or a lethal strike to your throat.

The best method for practicing your fighting stance is in front of a full-length mirror. Place the mirror in an area that allows sufficient room for movement; a garage or basement is perfect. Stand in front of the mirror, far enough away to see your entire body. Stand naturally with your arms relaxed at your sides. Now close your eyes and quickly assume your fighting stance. Open your eyes and check for flaws. Look for low hand guards, improper foot positioning or body angle, rigid shoulders and knees, etc. Drill this way repeatedly, working from both the right and left side. Practice this until your fighting stance becomes second nature.

The Fighting Stance

CHIN ANGLED DOWN

HANDS HELD UP

TORSO BLADED

ELBOWS TUCKED IN

KNEES BENT

FEET SHOULDER-WIDTH APART

FEET PARALLEL

Footwork & Mobility

Next are footwork and mobility. I define mobility as the ability to move your body quickly and freely, which is accomplished through basic footwork. The safest footwork involves quick, economical steps performed on the balls of your feet, while you remain relaxed and balanced. Keep in mind that balance is your most important consideration.

Basic footwork can be used for both offensive and defensive purposes, and it is structured around four general directions: forward, backward, right, and left. However, always remember this footwork rule of thumb: Always move the foot closest to the direction you want to go first, and let the other foot follow an equal distance. This prevents cross-stepping, which can cost you your life in a high-risk combat situation.

Basic Footwork Movements

1. Moving forward (advance) - from your fighting stance, first move your front foot forward (approximately 12 inches) and then move your rear foot an equal distance.

2. Moving backward (retreat) - from your fighting stance, first move your rear foot backward (approximately 12 inches) and then move your front foot an equal distance.

3. Moving right (sidestep right) - from your fighting stance, first move your right foot to the right (approximately 12 inches) and then move your left foot an equal distance.

4. Moving left (sidestep left) - from your fighting stance, first move your left foot to the left (approximately 12 inches) and then move your right foot an equal distance.

Practice these four movements for 10 to 15 minutes a day in front of a full-length mirror. In a couple weeks, your footwork should be quick, balanced, and natural.

Circling Right and Left

Strategic circling is an advanced form of footwork where you will use your front leg as a pivot point. This type of movement can also be used defensively to evade an overwhelming assault or to strike the opponent from various strategic angles. Strategic circling can be performed from either a left or right stance.

Circling left (from a left stance) - this means you'll be moving your body around the opponent in a clockwise direction. From a left stance, step 8 to 12 inches to the left with your left foot, then use your left leg as a pivot point and wheel your entire rear leg to the left until the correct stance and positioning is acquired.

Circling right (from a right stance) - from a right stance, step 8 to 12 inches to the right with your right foot, then use your right leg as a pivot point and wheel your entire rear leg to the right until the correct stance and positioning is acquired.

Combat Attributes

A kick, punch, block, or any fighting technique for that matter is useless unless it is accompanied by certain combative attributes. Attributes are qualities that enhance your particular body weapon or technique.

For example, speed, power, timing, non telegraphic movement, rhythm, coordination, accuracy, balance, and range specificity are just a few self-defense attributes that must be present if any technique or maneuver is to be effective in a high-risk self-defense situation.

Let's explore a few basic attributes necessary for fighting: speed, power, timing, balance, and non telegraphic movement.

Speed

To effectively land any offensive strike you must possess speed. By speed, I am referring to how fast your body weapon moves to its target. A fast technique should be likened to the strike of a snake. It should be felt and not seen by your assailant.

While some athletes are blessed with great speed, you should make every possible attempt to develop your speed to the maximum of your ability. One of the easiest ways of enhancing your speed is to simply relax your body prior to executing your body weapon. For example, when executing a palm heel strike to your assailant's chin, your arm should simply shoot straight out and back to its starting point without muscular tension. This may sound simple, but you'd be amazed how many people have difficulty relaxing—especially when they are under tremendous stress. Another way of developing blinding speed is to practice throwing all of your offensive weapons in the air. Focus on quickly executing and retracting your tool or technique as quickly as you can. If you are persistent and work diligently, you can achieve significant results.

Power

Power refers to the amount of impact force you can generate when striking your target. The power of your natural body weapon is not necessarily predicated on your size and strength. A relatively small person can generate devastating power if he or she combines it with sufficient speed. This explains why someone like Bruce Lee who weighed approximately 130 pounds could hit harder than most 200-pound men. Lee knew how to maximize his impact power through the speed at which he executed his techniques.

Ideally, when attempting to strike your assailant, you want to put your entire body behind your blow. I instruct my students to always aim 3 inches through their chosen target. Torquing your hips and shoulder into your blows will also help generate tremendous power. Remember, in a real self-defense situation, you want to hit your assailant with the power equivalent of a shotgun and not a squirt gun.

Timing

Timing refers to your ability to execute a technique or movement at the optimum moment. There are two types of timing: defensive and offensive. Defensive timing is the time between the assailant's attack and your defensive response to that attack. Offensive timing is the time between your recognition of a target opening and your offensive response to that opening.

Among the best ways of developing both offensive and defensive timing are stick and knife fighting, sparring sessions, double-end bag training, and various focus mitt drills. Mental visualization is also another effective method of enhancing timing. Visualizing various self-defense scenarios that require precise timing is ideal for enhancing your skills.

Balance

Effectively striking your assailant requires substantial follow-through while maintaining your balance. Balance is your ability to maintain equilibrium while stationary or moving. You can maintain perfect balance only through controlling your center of gravity, mastering body mechanics, and proper skeletal alignment.

To develop your sense of balance, perform your body weapons and techniques slowly so you become acquainted with the different weight distributions, body positions, and mechanics of each particular weapon. For example, when executing an elbow strike, keep your head, torso, legs, and feet in proper relation to each other. Be certain to follow through your target, but don't overextend yourself.

Non Telegraphic Movement

The element of surprise is an invaluable tool for self-defense. Successfully landing a blow requires that you do not forewarn your assailant of your intentions. Clenching your teeth, widening your eyes, cocking your fist, and tensing your neck or shoulders are just a few common telegraphic cues that will negate the element of surprise.

One of the best ways to prevent telegraphic movement is to maintain a poker face prior to executing your body weapon or technique. Avoid all facial expressions when faced with a threatening assailant. As mentioned, you can study your techniques and maneuvers in front of a full-length mirror or have a friend videotape you performing your movements. These procedures will assist you in identifying and ultimately eliminating telegraphic movements. Be patient and you'll reach your objective.

Tools and Techniques

If you want to be able to apply some of the attack methods discussed in the next chapter, you must have a working knowledge of your natural body weapons. Body weapons are simply the various parts of your body that can be used immediately as weapons to neutralize your adversary.

You have 14 natural body weapons at your disposal. They are easy to learn and, when properly executed, have the potential to disable, cripple, and even kill an attacker. They include the head, teeth, voice, elbows, fists, palms, fingers and nails, edge of hand, web of the hand, knees, shins, dorsum of the foot, heel of foot, and ball of foot.

An important point - contrary to some traditional martial arts - these body weapons do not require any preliminary hardening or conditioning exercises. Such archaic practices are unnecessary and can permanently damage and disfigure your limbs.

Head

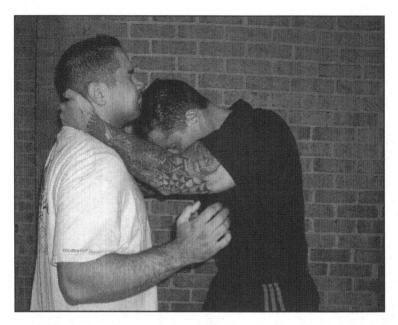

When you are fighting in close quarters, your head can be used for butting your assailant's nose. Head butts are ideal when a strong attacker has placed you in a hold where your arms are pinned against your sides. Keep in mind that the head butt can be delivered in four different directions: forward, backward, right side, and left side.

Teeth

The teeth can be used for biting anything on the assailant's body (nose, ears, throat, fingers, etc.). It is important, however, for you to muster the mental determination to bite deep and hard into the assailant's flesh and shake your head vigorously, much like a vicious dog killing his enemy. While this may seem primitive and barbaric, it is essential to your survival.

Although a bite is extremely painful, it also transmits a strong psychological message to your assailant. It lets him know that you, too, can be vicious and are willing to do anything to survive the encounter.

Warning: There is one important concern to biting tactics: you run the risk of contracting AIDS if your attacker is infected and you draw blood while biting him.

Elbows

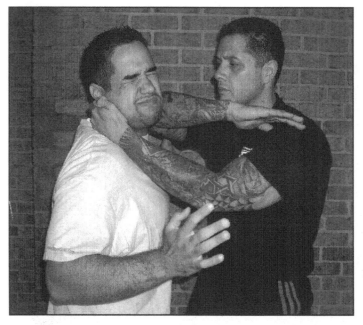

With very little training, you can learn to use your elbows as
devastating self-defense weapons. They are explosive, deceptive,
and difficult to stop. By rotating your body into the blow, you can
generate tremendous force. You can deliver elbow strikes horizontally,
vertically, and diagonally to the assailant's nose, temple, chin, throat,
solar plexus, and ribs.

Fists

The fists are used for punching an assailant's temple, nose, chin, throat, solar plexus, ribs, and groin. However, punching with your fists is a true art, requiring considerable time and training to master. Punching techniques include the lead straight, rear cross, hooks, upper cuts, shovel hooks, and hammer fists.

Fingers and Nails

Your fingers and nails can be used for jabbing, gouging, and clawing the opponent's eyes. They can also be used for grabbing, pulling, tearing, and crushing his throat or testicles.

Palms

One alternative to punching with your fists is to strike with the heel of your palm. A palm strike from either one of your hands is very powerful and should always be delivered in an upward, thrusting motion to the assailant's nose or chin.

Edge of the Hand

You can throw the edge of your hand in a whiplike motion to surprise and neutralize your attacker. By whipping your arm horizontally to his nose or throat, you can cause severe injury or death. The edge of your hand can also be thrown vertically or diagonally to the back of the assailant's neck as a finishing blow.

Web of the Hand

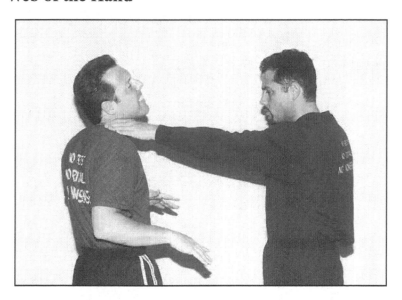

The web of your hand can be used to deliver web hand strikes to the opponent's throat. When striking, be certain to keep your hand stiff with your palm facing down.

Knees

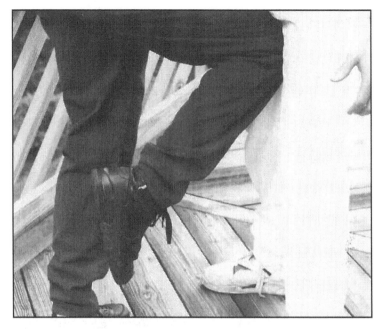

When you are fighting the opponent in close-quarter grappling range, your knees can be extremely powerful weapons. You can deliver knee strikes vertically and diagonally to the assailant's thigh and groin, ribs, solar plexus, and face.

Shins

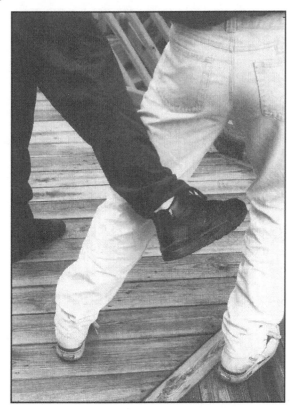

Striking with your shinbone can quickly cripple a powerful assailant and bring him to his knees in agony. That's right—your shinbone is a weapon. When striking with your shin, you can aim for his thigh, the side of his knee, or groin—and always remember to aim through your target.

Dorsum of Foot

You can use the dorsum of your foot to execute a vertical kick to the assailant's groin, and in some cases, his head. Striking with the dorsum increases the power of your kick, prevents broken toes, and also lengthens the surface area of your strike.

Heel of the Foot

You can use the heel of your foot to execute a side kick to the opponent's knee or shin. When fighting an attacker in grappling range, you can use the heel of your foot to stomp down on the assailant's instep or toes.

Ball of the Foot

You can use the ball of your foot to execute a push kick into the assailant's thigh. You can also snap it quickly into the assailant's shin to loosen a grab from the front. When striking the assailant with the ball of your foot, be certain to pull your toes back to avoid jamming or breaking them.

Anatomical Targets

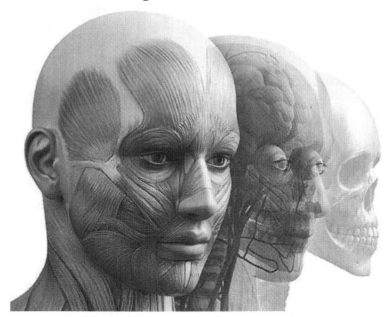

Knowing how and when to strike your attacker is essential; however knowing where to hit him is equally important. Anyone who is seriously interested in neutralizing a formidable assailant must have a working knowledge and understanding of the body targets on the human anatomy. This is called target orientation.

Many people don't realize that the human body has many structural weaknesses that are especially vulnerable to attack. The human body simply was not designed to take the punishment of strikes and blows. Always keep in mind that regardless of your attacker's size, strength, or state of mind, he will always have vulnerable targets that can be attacked.

Unfortunately, very little information has been written on anatomical targets and the medical implications of self-defense strikes. Every martial artist, self-defense expert, combat specialist, and law enforcement officer has a moral and legal responsibility to know the medical implications of strikes and techniques. It is your responsibility to know which targets will stun, incapacitate, disfigure, cripple, or kill your assailant. Knowledge of the medical implications will also make you a more efficient technician.

I am astonished by some martial art and self-defense instructors who teach ineffective targets. For example, the biceps, collar bone, kidneys, coronal suture, or Achilles tendon are just a few targets that yield poor results when struck. Such anatomical targets won't neutralize a vicious opponent immediately. In many cases, it will only anger him and provoke him to attack with greater viciousness and determination. Therefore, it is essential that you strike targets that will immediately incapacitate the opponent. Anything less can get you severely injured or killed. Don't forget this point.

For practical purposes you only need to know a handful of anatomical targets. We will focus on 13 vulnerable targets categorized into three zones.

The 3 Target Zones

For reasons of clarity, we can categorize both the primary and secondary anatomical targets into one of three possible zones.

Zone 1 (Head region) consists of targets related to your senses. This includes: the eyes, temples, nose, chin, and back of neck.

Zone 2 (Neck, Torso, Groin) consists of targets related to breathing. This includes: the throat, solar plexus, ribs, and testicles.

Zone 3 (Legs, Feet) consists of targets related to mobility. This includes: the thighs, knees, shins, instep, and toes.

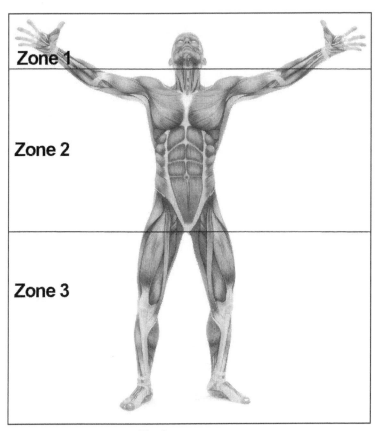

The three target zones.

EYES

Eyes sit in the orbital bones of the skull. They are ideal targets for self-defense because they are extremely sensitive and difficult to protect, and striking them requires very little force. The eyes can be poked, scratched,

and gouged from a variety of angles. Depending on the force of your strike, it can cause numerous injuries, including watering of the eyes, hemorrhaging, blurred vision, temporary or permanent blindness, severe pain, rupture, shock, and unconsciousness.

NOSE

The nose is made up of a thin bone, cartilage, numerous blood vessels, and many nerves. It is a particularly good target because it stands out from the opponent's face and can be struck from three different directions (up, straight, down). A moderate blow can cause stunning pain, eye-watering, temporary blindness, and hemorrhaging. A powerful strike can result in shock and unconsciousness.

CHIN

In boxing, the chin is considered a "knockout button," responsible for retiring hundreds of boxers. The chin is equally a good target for self-defense. When it is struck at a

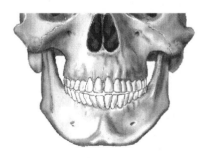

45-degree angle, shock is transmitted to the cerebellum and cerebral hemispheres of the brain, resulting in paralysis and immediate unconsciousness. Other possible injuries include broken jaw, concussion, and whiplash to the neck.

TEMPLE

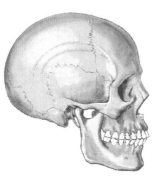

The temple or sphenoid bone is a thin, weak bone located on the side of the skull approximately 1 inch from the eyes. Because of its fragile structure and close proximity to the brain, a powerful strike to this target can be deadly. Other injuries include unconsciousness, hemorrhage, concussion, shock, and coma.

THROAT

The throat is a lethal target because it is only protected by a thin layer of skin. This region consists of the thyroid, hyaline and crocoid cartilage, trachea, and larynx. The trachea, or windpipe, is a cartilaginous tube that measures 4 1/2 inches in length and is approximately 1 inch in diameter. A powerful strike to this target can result in unconsciousness, blood drowning, massive hemorrhaging, air starvation, and death. If the thyroid cartilage is crushed, hemorrhaging will occur, the windpipe will quickly swell shut, resulting in suffocation.

GROIN

Everyone man will agree that the genitals are highly sensitive organs. Even a light strike can be debilitating. A moderate strike to the groin can result in severe pain, nausea, vomiting, shortness of breath, and possible sterility. A powerful blow to the groin can crush the scrotum and testes against the pubic bones, causing shock and unconsciousness.

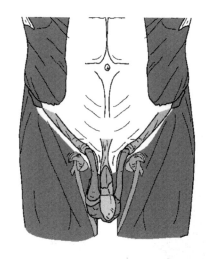

THIGHS

Many people don't realize that the thighs are also vulnerable targets. A moderate kick to the rectus femoris or vastus lateralis muscles will result in immediate immobility of the leg. An extremely hard kick to the thigh can result in a fracture of the femur, resulting in internal bleeding, severe pain, cramping, and immobility of the broken leg.

BACK OF NECK

The back of the neck consists of the first seven vertebrae of the spinal column. They act as a circuit board for nerve impulses from the brain to the body. The back of the neck is a lethal target because the vertebrae are poorly protected. A very powerful strike to the back of the neck can cause shock, 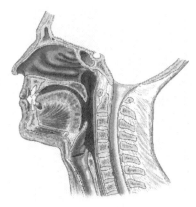 unconsciousness, a broken neck, complete paralysis, coma, and death.

RIBS

There are 12 pair of ribs in the human body. Excluding the eleventh and twelfth ribs, they are long and slender bones that are joined by the vertebral column in the back and the sternum and costal cartilage in the front.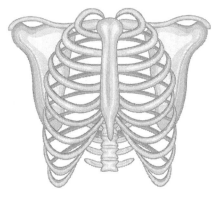

Since there are no eleventh and twelfth ribs (floating ribs) in the front, you should direct your strikes to the ninth and tenth ribs. A moderate strike to the anterior region of the ribs will cause severe pain and shortness of breath. A powerful 45-degree blow could easily break a rib and force it into a lung, resulting in its collapse, internal hemorrhaging, severe pain, air starvation, unconsciousness, and possible death.

SOLAR PLEXUS

The solar plexus is a large collection of nerves situated below the sternum in the upper abdomen. A moderate blow to this area will cause nausea, tremendous pain, and shock, making it difficult for the assailant to breathe. A powerful strike to the solar plexus can result in severe abdominal pain and cramping, air starvation, and shock.

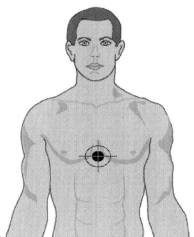

KNEES

The knee connects the femur to the tibia. It is a very weak joint held together by a number of supporting ligaments. When the assailant's leg is locked or fixed and a forceful strike is delivered to the front of the joint, the cruciate ligaments will tear, resulting in excruciating pain, swelling, and immobility.

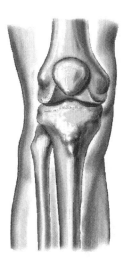

Located on the front of the knee joint is the patella, which is made of a small, loose piece of bone. The patella is also extremely vulnerable to dislocation by a direct, forceful kick. Severe pain, swelling, and immobility will quickly result.

SHINS

Everyone, at one time or another, has knocked his or her shin bone into the end of a table or bed accidentally and felt the intense pain associated with it. The shin is very sensitive because the bone is only protected by a thin layer of skin. However, a powerful kick delivered to this target can easily fracture it, resulting in nauseating pain, hemorrhaging, and immobility.

FINGERS

The fingers or digits are considered weak and vulnerable targets that can easily be jammed, sprained, broken, torn, and bitten. While a broken finger might not stop an attacker, it will certainly make him release his hold. A broken finger also makes it difficult for the assailant to clench his fist or hold a weapon. When attempting to break an assailant's finger, it's best to grab the pinkie and forcefully tear backward against the knuckle.

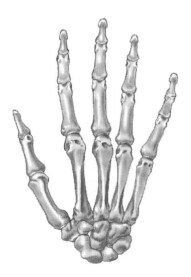

TOES/INSTEP

With a powerful stomp of your heel, you can break the small bones of an assailant's toes and or instep, causing severe pain and immobility. Stomping on the toes is an excellent technique for releasing many holds. It should be mentioned, however, that you should avoid an attack to the toes/instep if the attacker is wearing hard leather boots, i.e., combat, hiking, or motorcycle boots.

Bruce Lee's 5 Methods of Attack

What follows is a list of ineffective anatomical targets that yield poor results when struck in a street fight. NOTE: This list does not apply to firearms, stick or knife combat.

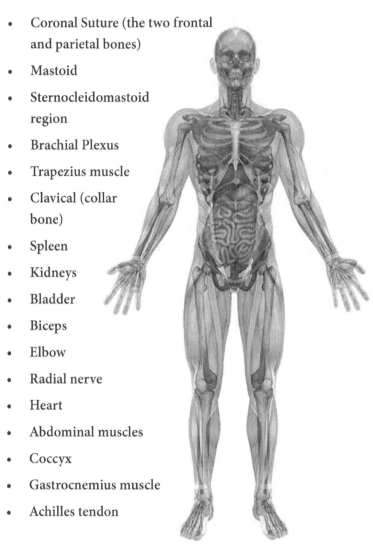

- Coronal Suture (the two frontal and parietal bones)
- Mastoid
- Sternocleidomastoid region
- Brachial Plexus
- Trapezius muscle
- Clavical (collar bone)
- Spleen
- Kidneys
- Bladder
- Biceps
- Elbow
- Radial nerve
- Heart
- Abdominal muscles
- Coccyx
- Gastrocnemius muscle
- Achilles tendon

Chapter Three
The Five Methods of Attack

The Methods of Attack

As I discussed in the preface, Bruce Lee cataloged five methods of attack. These methods are classified as follows:

- **Attack by Drawing (ABD)**
- **Hand Immobilization Attack (HIA)**
- **Progressive Indirect Attack (PIA)**
- **Simple Angular Attack (SAA)**
- **Attack By Combination (ABC)**

As I stated earlier, while each method is unique in strategic concept, not all of them are suitable for high-risk self-defense situations. Some are defensive in concept while other depend upon unreliable variables and factors. Recognizing the dangers and limitations in some of these attack methods could mean the difference between life and death in a street fight.

NOTE: By assessing the practical implications of the five methods of attack and pointing out strategic weaknesses, I don't wish to discredit Bruce Lee and his work. To the contrary, he was a clever innovator who was years ahead of his time. Nevertheless, my goal is to distinguish methods appropriate for real world self-defense from methods which should be restricted to safe and relatively predictable environments of the gym or dojo. Having said that, let's begin with the Attack By Drawing (ABD) methodology.

Just because a particular technique worked for Bruce Lee, doesn't necessarily mean it would work for the average person. Bruce Lee was an exceptionally gifted individual who possessed incredible speed, power and timing.

Attack by Drawing (ABD)

"The attack by drawing is an attack or counterattack initiated upon luring the opponent into a commitment by leaving him an apparent opening or executing movements that he may try to time and counter. Attack by drawing may make use of the other four ways of attack. Study timing and the eight basic defense positions."

-Bruce Lee, Tao of Jeet Kune Do

Attack by drawing is counter fighting. In this method of attack, the martial artist offers the opponent an enticing bait (i. e. an intentional opening designed to lure an attack). A common drawing technique is wide hand positioning, as if to say, "Come on, take your best shot!" Once the opponent takes the bait, the practitioner swiftly executes a preplanned and perfectly timed counter attack. Proponents of this attack method argue that it forces the opponent to commit himself to a decided action and offers you the opportunity to observe his style of fighting.

Attack by Drawing Demonstration

Step1: The man on the right squares off with his opponent and offers a wide hand positioning to draw an attack.

Step 2: The opponent exploits the opening by initiating a jab.

Step 3: The defender immediately parries the attack and counters with a back fist strike to the face.

While the Attack by Drawing (ABD) method may be safe to use under sparring conditions, it poses dangerous problems in a real fight. In such a dangerous situation, who's to say you'll be able to stop, intercept or counter the opponent's initial attack. For example, suppose he has exceptional hand speed. Or, what if the adversary seizes your intentional opening as an opportunity to initiate a deceptive and relentless flurry of devastating blows? You could easily find yourself in an irreversible defensive flow that could get you severely injured or possibly killed in the streets.

Just because you create a vacant opening in a fight, doesn't guarantee the opponent will take the bait. Many opponents will have a single-minded agenda regardless of what you present to them in a fight.

Bruce Lee's 5 Methods of Attack

The bottom line is under no circumstances should you allow the opponent to gain the advantage of initiating the first strike in a real fight. Frankly, it's like allowing a gunslinger to draw his weapon first. If he's accurate and hits his target, it's light out for you!

Once it is clear that you will be attacked, or that a fight is unavoidable, you should do everything in your power to take control the situation. This means strike first, strike fast, strike with authority, and keep the pressure on.

This offensive strategy is known as my first-strike principle, and it's essential to the process of neutralizing a formidable adversary in a high-risk self-defense altercation. A first strike is defined as the strategic application of proactive force designed to interrupt the initial stages of an assault before it becomes a full-blown self-defense situation.

One inescapable fact about street self-defense is that the longer the fight lasts, the greater your chances of serious injury or even death. Common sense suggests that you must end the fight as quickly as possible. Striking first is the best method of achieving this tactical objective because it permits you to neutralize your assailant swiftly while, at the same time, precluding his ability to retaliate effectively. No time is wasted, and no unnecessary risks are taken.

When it comes to reality based self-defense, the element of surprise is invaluable. Launching the first strike gives you the upper hand because it allows you to hit the adversary suddenly and unexpectedly. As a result, you demolish his defenses and ultimately take him out of the fight.

Ultimately, the best defense is a powerful and overwhelming offense. I agree that deception is a key factor in all forms of combat, however, the attack by drawing method (ABD) is a gamble you should never take on the street.

Hand Immobilization Attack (HIA)

"The immobilization attack is performed by applying an immobilizing preparation (trapping) on the opponent's head (hair), hand or legs as you crash the line to engagement. The trapping keeps the opponent from moving that part of his body, offering you a safety zone and from which to strike. Immobilization attacks can be prepared (set-up) by using any of the other four ways of attack and traps can be performed in combination or singularly."

-Bruce Lee, Tao of Jeet Kune Do

Trapping is a highly complex system of moves and counter moves designed to control the opponent's limb(s) in order to execute an offense attack. Trapping techniques may be applied against arms and hands or legs. Generally, however, the more intricate trapping techniques involve the upper gates, i.e., the arms and hands. Trapping requires lightning-quick reflexes and highly developed

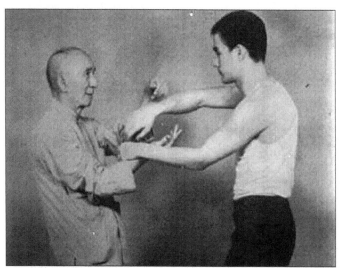

Picture here, Bruce Lee and his teacher Yip Man performing Chi Sao, an energy and sensitivity drill that improves hand trapping skills.

tactile sensitivity. It truly is an impressive sight to watch two really accomplish trappers go at it. However, aesthetics do not dictate the outcome of the vicious and potentially deadly street fight.

Effective trapping techniques are based on the opponent presenting a proper structure for response. His hands must accept the trappers initiating feed in just the right way. The trapping feed can either be a linear or circular attack to engage the opponent's counter or guard. Once the initial lockup takes place the trapper can go to work with close-quarter strikes, parries, locks, energy reversals and other techniques aimed at neutralizing the opponent and gaining further openings. All of this may sound impressive but for the street it can be disastrous. As I said before, just because this method of attack worked for Bruce Lee, doesn't necessarily mean it will work for you.

Pictured here, the trapping range of unarmed combat.

The truth is you simply cannot rely on your opponent presenting the predefined structure necessary for various trapping techniques. For example, if your "feeds" are not adequately engaged by the opponent, you can't build a trapping structure. If the opponent disengages - which is extremely likely in a real fighting situation - the trap disintegrates. Worse yet, the opponent can easily counter the lockup with a series of head butts, elbows, knee strikes and body tackles.

Some proponents of trapping argue that it's a by-product of hitting. They say that you should hit before and after every trap, and you should only trap when your strike is obstructed. However, in the real world, combat is frenzied and unpredictable. In some ways, it's likened to a gruesome car wreck. In almost all cases your adversary will be fueled by blood-thirsty rage and pure adrenaline. He simply won't offer you the static and controlled defensive structure necessary for effective trapping techniques.

There are simply too many uncertainties and variables to trapping. These techniques are based on assumptions you cannot afford to make in a high risk self-defense situation. Finally, trapping too often results in a grappling situation which invariably ends up on the ground. This is the last place you want to be in a street fight. The bottom line is – leave trapping in the gym or dojo. Don't take it to the streets.

If you're still determined to keep trapping techniques in your fighting arsenal, consider using it strictly for attribute development.

Hand Immobilization Attack Demonstration

Step 1: Franco (right) creates an attachment with is lead hand.

Step 2: Next, Franco builds on the trap with a parry (pak sao) and a lead vertical punch to his opponent's face. His opponent parries his punch.

Step 3: Once the opponent's parrying hand crosses his centerline, Franco delivers a rear vertical punch to the face.

Step 4: Franco grabs his opponent's wrist with his left hand and strikes with his right hand.

In the streets, your adversary will most likely be fueled by rage and adrenaline. He simply won't offer you the calm and controlled defensive structure necessary for effective trapping techniques.

Progressive Indirect Attack (PIA)

"The progressive indirect attack is preceded by a feint or an uncommitted thrust designed to misdirect the opponent's actions or reactions in order to hit the opening line or gain a period of movement – time. The progressive indirect attack is performed in a single forward motion without a withdrawal, as opposed to the single angulated attack preceded by a feint which is actually two movements."

-Bruce Lee, Tao of Jeet Kune Do

The indirect attack is progressive in nature. It always involves more than one offense technique. Do not, however, confuse the indirect attack with its superior cousin, the compound attack.

The indirect attack builds through stages. The initial techniques is not the coup de grace, i.e., the knockout weapon. In fact, in many indirect attacks the initiating technique is not even the weapon, but one of any number of feints or other deceptions designed to open the opponent up for the follow-up blow. Even when the initial technique is an actual kick, punch or any other striking tool, it serves merely as a set-up for the finishing blow.

In competition, the initiating technique sets up or accumulates valuable points, wears down the opponent, and opens them up to more devastating blows. The progressive indirect attack can also be very effective under sparring conditions. In real combat, however, where points are of no consequence and setups are not safe, the progressive indirect attack should not be employed.

In the explosive and dangerous situation of a real street fight, the martial artist cannot afford the risk of a setup technique. Any initiating strike delivered with less than maximum speed and force may likely be ignored and will certainly be countered with viciousness. Consider the sheer lunacy of attempting a feint against an opponent such as professional boxer. You cannot afford to gamble that your adversary will react in the manner intended.

Those who have trained excessively in the use of feints, should limit their use to closing the distance gap from a neutral distance. A feint from the neutral range does not create a risk as it would in any of the three ranges of unarmed combat. If the opponent fails to take the bait or reacts offensively, you're still at a relatively safe distance. Never use a feint in a range of engagement, i.e., kicking, punching, or grappling range. Feints from these ranges run the risk of an offense counter allowing the opponent to get the upper hand and thereby

The progressive indirect attack is great for sparring. In fact, I often encourage my students to use this methodology to confuse their sparring partners and add variety to their training.

placing you in the defensive flow.

Simply put, assumptions and experimentation in the face of danger are invitations to disaster! The progressive indirect attack involves too much risk and uncertainty. It lacks the all-out explosiveness, power and commitment required in the face of an attack by an opponent hell-bent on your destruction. Remember, in a high-risk self-defense situation no rules apply. Your subject to an attack from anywhere and anything. You cannot allow a dangerous assailant even the slightest opportunity get the upper hand.

Never forget that sparring does not represent the violent dynamics and real danger of a vicious street fight. Remember, sparring is nothing more than a training methodology used to develop combat attributes.

Progressive Indirect Attack Demonstration

Step 1: Two men square off in fighting stances.

Step 2: The man on the left begins his indirect attack with a low line fake.

Step 3: The opponent goes for the fake by parrying down with his left hand. The man on the left builds on his indirect attack with a lead hook to the opening.

Simple Angular Attack (SAA)

"The simple angle attack is any simple attack thrown at a unexpected angle, sometimes preceded by feinting. It is often set up by readjusting the distance with footwork."

-Bruce Lee, Tao of Jeet Kune Do

The simple angle attack (SAA) is also called the simple direct attack (SDA). In this method, the martial artist delivers a solitary offense technique. It may involve a series of discrete probes or one swift and powerful strike aimed at terminating the encounter. Whatever the strategy, the simple angle attack and simple direct attack is predicated entirely upon one isolated strike.

Some proponents of this method argue that it is the safest attack because it does not require full commitment to the opponent. Others proclaim it to be the highest form of attack when one swift, powerful blow dictates the outcome of the fight.

Here, Sammy Franco (right) demonstrates the simple direct attack.

Bruce Lee's 5 Methods of Attack

First, in a real fight, what possible sense does it make to remain uncommitted to the adversary? The fact is, you cannot effectively neutralize a formidable aggressor by lingering at the perimeter of the encounter. Rather than toying with probes and other isolated "feelers," you must commit yourself 100% with the most powerful and effective flow of tools appropriate to the targets, ranges, and openings.

Furthermore, you cannot afford the risk that one perfectly executed punch, palm heel strike, kick or other technique will terminate the fight. It's not that it can't be done. It's just that single strike victories are few and far between. They are the rare luxury of the highly trained and skilled martial artist – and even then, it sometimes requires a little luck.

To drive the point home, think of the now familiar law enforcement stories of drug-induced criminal aggressors who keep coming after being hit by a .38 caliber bullet. There are a lot of those types of people out there and they're often involved in violent street attacks.

Pictured here, the single attack in punching range.

The bottom line is, unless you are Bruce Lee, you cannot rely on the simple attack to stop such a dangerous assailant. In almost every case you won't know your aggressor's pain tolerance, state of mind or capability for violence.

However, there's nothing wrong with developing the capability to knock your opponent out with a single blow. In fact, every serious martial artist should have a few knock-out techniques in his or her arsenal. Here are a few ways you can develop bone-shattering power.

Proficiency Training on the Heavy Bag

Proficiency training is generally used by martial artists and self-defense practitioners who want to sharpen one specific punch, kick, or strike at a time by executing it over and over for a prescribed number of repetitions. Each time the technique is performed with "clean" form at various speeds. Punches are also carried out with the eyes closed to develop a kinesthetic "feel" for the action.

Technique Isolation Training

Technique Isolation training is a variation of the proficiency training methodology. The purpose of this exercise is to focus exclusively on one specific punch (i.e., lead straight, rear cross, lead hook, etc.) for your entire workout. For example, if you wanted to sharpen and develop your lead straight punch, you would isolate and practice it exclusively on the heavy bag for a specified number of rounds.

"I fear not the man who has practiced 10,000 kicks once, but I fear the man who has practiced one kick 10,000 times." -Bruce Lee

Isolation Training (Lead Straight) Demonstration

Step 1: The practitioner assumes a fighting stance.

Step 2: He delivers a high lead straight at the bag.

Step 3: He begins circling the bag in a clockwise direction.

Step 4: He throws a low lead straight.

Step 5: As he moves around the bag, he throws another high punch.

Step 6: Next, another low punch.

Step 7: Followed by a high lead straight punch.

Step 8: He delivers another low punch and continues to circle around the heavy bag.

Step 9: He fires off another high punch.

Step 10: The practitioner continues punching and moving around the at the bag for a duration of 3 minutes.

Technique Isolation Workout Routines

Skill Level	Duration of Each Round	Rest Period	Total Number of rounds
Beginner	1 minute	2 minutes	3
Beginner	1 minute	1 minute	3
Beginner	2 minutes	2 minutes	3
Beginner	2 minutes	1 minute	3
Intermediate	3 minutes	2 minutes	5
Intermediate	3 minutes	1 minute	5
Intermediate	3 minutes	2 minutes	6
Intermediate	3 minutes	1 minute	6
Advanced	4 minutes	2 minutes	8
Advanced	4 minutes	1 minute	8
Advanced	5 minutes	2 minutes	10
Advanced	5 minutes	1 minute	10

In order to maximize the full benefit of technique isolation training, it's important to stick to only one punch for your entire workout. For example, if you're a beginner who wants to perfect your jab, you would practice it exclusively for a total of 3 rounds.

Elevation Drill

If you are looking to develop knock-out punching power, look no further than the elevation drill. In fact, this is one of the most demanding exercises you can perform on the heavy bag. Besides requiring a tremendous amount of muscular endurance, the drill also requires a significant amount of mental resilience and attention control.

The objective of this exercise is to keep the heavy bag elevated at a 45-degree angle by continuously punching it. This drill is brutal on the arms. In fact, the average person can barely last 30 seconds. To perform the drill follow these steps:

1. Face the heavy bag and assume a fighting stance.

2. Deliver the jab and rear cross combination continuously. Concentrate on delivering full-speed, full-force punches.

3. Maintain a rapid-fire cadence to keep the bag elevated at a 45-degree angle from the floor.

4. Avoid pushing the bag and remember to snap each blow. If the heavy bag spins when performing this exercise, it means your punches are not landing at the center of the bag. Remember to focus your blows at a single target point.

5. Perform the drill for a minimum of three rounds. Each round can last anywhere from 10 to 90 seconds. If you are exceptionally conditioned, go for 90 seconds.

The goal of the elevation drill is to keep the heavy bag elevated at approximately 45-degrees by continuously punching it.

Be very careful when performing this exercise. One misplaced punch or bent wrist can easily lead to a severe injury.

Elevation Drill Demonstration

Step 1: The practitioner assumes a fighting stance.

Step 2: He begins with a powerful lead straight punch.

Step 3: He immediately follows with a rear cross.

Step 4: Next, another lead straight punch.

Step 5: The speed and power of the blows elevate the heavy bag at a 45-degree angle.

Step 6: To keep the bag elevated at 45-degrees, the practitioner must continue to attack the heavy bag with vicious intent.

Step 7: The practitioner delivers another rapid-fire rear across.

Step 8: Followed by another powerful lead punch.

Step 9: The practitioner continues his barrage for a total of 60 seconds.

While the elevation drill is strictly designed for developing linear punching power, it's also a great methodology for developing mental toughness.

Elevation Drill Workout Routines

Skill Level	Duration of Each Round	Rest Period	Total Number of rounds
Beginner	10 seconds	2 minutes	3
Beginner	15 seconds	1 minute	3
Beginner	20 seconds	2 minutes	3
Beginner	25 minutes	1 minute	3
Intermediate	30 seconds	2 minutes	5
Intermediate	35 seconds	1 minute	5
Intermediate	40 seconds	2 minutes	5
Intermediate	45 seconds	1 minute	5
Advanced	60 seconds	2 minutes	6
Advanced	70 seconds	1 minute	6
Advanced	80 seconds	2 minutes	6
Advanced	90 seconds	1 minute	6

Cyclone Drill

The Cyclone Drill develops is designed to develop bone-crushing hook punches. The objective of the exercise is to assault the heavy bag with a continuous flurry of hook punches delivered in a back and forth fashion. This drill also permits you to strike both high and low heavy bag targets. To perform the Cyclone drill, follow these steps:

1. Face the heavy bag and assume a fighting stance.

2. Deliver the lead and rear hook punches in a fluid, back and forth fashion. Concentrate on striking the bag as fast and hard as possible.

3. Perform the drill for a minimum of three rounds. Each round can last anywhere from 10 to 90 seconds.

Cyclone Drill Demonstration

Step 1: The practitioner throws a high lead hook punch at the bag.

Step 2: Next, a rear hook.

Step 3: Followed by a lead hook.

Step 4: He continues with a rear hook.

Step 5: Then another high lead hook punch.

Step 6: The practitioner continues his assault for a total of 30 seconds.

Cyclone Drill Workout Routines			
Skill Level	Duration of Each Round	Rest Period	Total Number of rounds
Beginner	10 seconds	2 minutes	3
Beginner	15 seconds	1 minute	3
Beginner	20 seconds	2 minutes	3
Beginner	25 minutes	1 minute	3
Intermediate	30 seconds	2 minutes	5
Intermediate	35 seconds	1 minute	5
Intermediate	40 seconds	2 minutes	5
Intermediate	45 seconds	1 minute	5
Advanced	60 seconds	2 minutes	6
Advanced	70 seconds	1 minute	6
Advanced	80 seconds	2 minutes	6
Advanced	90 seconds	1 minute	6

"Punch-a Hole" Exercise

Any boxer worth his salt will tell you that heavy bag training is a delicate mixture of power, speed, timing, and pacing. However, the real secret to making it through a full three-minute round on the heavy bag is to pace the power of your strikes.

Some of you might already know that full force, full speed punching will invariably lead to a very short-lived training round. In most instances, the average person can only sustain "all out" power punching for approximately 30 seconds. That's also assuming they are punching with proper form.

The "Punch a Hole" exercise goes against this conventional wisdom by training you to hit the bag as hard as humanly possible. In essence, your goal is to literally try and punch a hole through the heavy bag. Is this actually possible? I seriously doubt it! Nevertheless, this type of training will transform your fists into virtual sledgehammers.

"Punch a Hole" Workout Demonstration

Step 1: The practitioner assumes a fighting stance.

Step 2: He throws a rear cross punch.

Step 3: Next, he follows up with a strong lead straight punch.

Step 4: He drives a powerful low rear uppercut.

Step 5: A high lead hook punch.

Step 6: Followed by a bone-shattering rear cross.

Step 7: Another explosive lead punch.

Step 8: The practitioner continues his assault for a total of 30 seconds.

Beginner Level
"Punch a Hole" Workout Routines

Workout Routine	Duration of Each Round	Rest Period	Total Number of rounds
1	10 seconds	2 minutes	3
2	10 seconds	1 minute	3
3	15 seconds	2 minutes	3
4	15 seconds	1 minute	3
5	20 seconds	2 minutes	3
6	20 seconds	1 minute	3
7	25 seconds	2 minutes	3
8	25 seconds	1 minute	3
9	10 seconds	1 minute	5
10	15 seconds	2 minutes	5
11	20 seconds	1 minute	5
12	25 seconds	2 minutes	5

The "punch a hole" drill requires you to hit the bag as hard as possible! Do not perform this exercise unless you are absolutely certain you have mastered the proper body mechanics of punching.

	Intermediate Level "Punch a Hole" Workout Routines		
Workout Routine	Duration of Each Round	Rest Period	Total Number of rounds
1	30 seconds	2 minutes	3
2	30 seconds	1 minute	3
3	35 seconds	2 minutes	3
4	35 seconds	1 minute	3
5	40 seconds	2 minutes	3
6	40 seconds	1 minute	3
7	45 seconds	2 minutes	3
8	45 seconds	1 minute	3
9	30 seconds	1 minute	5
10	35 seconds	2 minutes	5
11	40 seconds	1 minute	5
12	45 seconds	2 minutes	5

Performing this drill for a duration of 30-45 seconds might not seem like a lot. However, I can assure you that after 5 rounds you will be thoroughly exhausted.

Advanced Level
"Punch a Hole" Workout Routines

Workout Routine	Duration of Each Round	Rest Period	Total Number of rounds
1	50 seconds	2 minutes	4
2	50 seconds	1 minute	4
3	55 seconds	2 minutes	4
4	55 seconds	1 minute	4
5	60 seconds	2 minutes	5
6	60 seconds	1 minute	5
7	65 seconds	2 minutes	5
8	65 seconds	1 minute	5
9	50 seconds	1 minute	6
10	55 seconds	2 minutes	6
11	60 seconds	1 minute	6
12	65 seconds	2 minutes	6

Performing this drill for a duration of 60 seconds or longer is generally reserved for professional fighters who want peak combat performance.

Attack By Combination (ABC)

"The attack by combination is a series of thrusts that follow each other naturally and are generally prone to more than one line."

-Bruce Lee, Tao of Jeet Kune Do

Attack by combination is also called a compound attack. A compound attack is any sequence of two or more tools launched in succession. However, it is significantly different from all the other methods of attack. It does not build through progressive stages; no time is wasted, and no unnecessary risks are taken.

Attack by combination has nothing to do with experimentation or assumptions. Rather, the martial artist gains the upper hand by initiating a flurry of strategically placed full-force, full-speed strikes designed to overwhelm the opponent's defenses. The ultimate objective is to take the fight out to the opponent and the opponent out of the fight.

Based on power, accuracy, speed and commitment, the compound attack also requires calculation, control and clarity. In other words, the unskilled, untrained brawler who goes off with a buzzsaw of violent strikes is not executing a compound attack. There is more to it than that.

The compound attack starts with a thorough understanding and knowledge of every conceivable anatomical target presented by the various stances, angles, distances, and movements of the opponent. Unless he is in full body armor, there are always targets. It is a question of recognizing them and striking quickly with the appropriate tools. This requires mastery of a wide range of offensive techniques, a complete understanding of combat ranges, reaction dynamic awareness, and the proper use of force.

But remember, what is universally true for all opponents is equally true for you. If there is always a target available on him, there's always one on you – although vulnerability can be reduced with proper martial arts training. Remember, strike first, strike fast, strike with authority, and keep the pressure on.

As you attack one target, others open up naturally. It is up to you to recognize them through reaction dynamic awareness and keep the offensive flow. Executed properly, the compound attack demolishes your opponents defenses that you ultimately take him down and out. It sounds great, but you must realize that it has to happen within seconds.

Probable Reaction Dynamics (PRD)

In my book, *Maximum Damage: Hidden Secrets Behind Brutal Fighting Combinations*, I define probable reaction dynamics as the opponent's anticipated or predicted movements or actions that occur in both armed and unarmed combat. Probable reaction dynamics will always be the result or residual of your initial action, i.e., punch, kick, push, grab, etc.

The most basic example of probable reaction dynamics can be illustrated by the following scenario. Let's say, you are fighting with your adversary and the opportunity presents itself to forcefully kick him in his groin. When your foot comes in contact with its target, your opponent will exhibit one of several "possible" physical or psychological reactions to your strike. These responses might include:

- The opponent's head and body violently drop forward.

- The opponent grabs or covers his groin region.

- The opponent struggles for breath.

- The opponent momentarily freezes.

- The opponent goes into shock.

Pictured here, a probable reaction dynamic to an eye strike.

Knowledge of your assailant's probable reaction dynamics is vital in both armed and unarmed combat. In fact, you must be mindful of the possible reaction dynamics to every kick, punch, strike, and technique in your arsenal. This is exactly what I refer to as *"reaction dynamic awareness"* and I can assure you this is not such an easy task. However, with proper training, it can be developed.

Regardless of your style of fighting (karate, muay thai, krav maga, boxing or mixed martial arts), understanding and ultimately mastering reaction dynamic awareness will give you a tremendous advantage in a fight by maximizing the effectiveness, efficiency and safety of your compound attack.

Flow like Water!

When you proceed with the compound attack, always maintain the offensive flow. The offensive flow is a progression of continuous offensive movements designed to neutralize your opponent. The key is to have each strike flow smoothly and efficiently from one to the next without causing you to lose ground. Subjecting your adversary to an offensive flow is especially effective because it taxes his nervous system, thereby dramatically lengthening his defensive reaction time.

In a real-life street fight it's critical that you always keep the offensive pressure on until your opponent is completely neutralized. Always remember that letting your offensive flow stagnate, even for a second, will open you up to numerous dangers and risks.

Proper breathing is another substantial element of the compound attack, and there is one simple rule that should be followed: exhale during the execution phase of your strike and inhale during its retraction phase. Above all, never hold your breath when delivering several consecutive blows. Doing so could lead to dizziness and fainting, among other complications.

Probable reaction dynamics will always be the result or residual of your initial action. This action can be in the form of a verbal statement, physical technique, or simple gesture directed at your opponent.

Time is a Factor!

Your body can only sustain delivering a compound attack for so long. Initially, your brain will quickly release adrenaline or epinephrine into your blood stream, which will fuel your fighting and enhance your strength and power. This lethal boost of energy is known as an adrenaline dump. However, your ability to exert and maintain this maximum effort in a compound attack will last no more than 30 to 60 seconds if you are in above-average shape. If the fight continues after that, your strength and speed may drop by as much as 50 percent below normal. When all is said and done, you don't have much time in a fight, so the battle needs to be won fast before your energy runs out!

Don't Forget to Relocate

Subsequent to your compound attack, immediately move to a new location by flanking your adversary. This tactic is known as relocating. The best way to accomplish this is through circling footwork. Based on the principles of strategy, movement, and surprise, relocating dramatically enhances your safety by making it difficult for your adversary to identify your position after you have attacked him. Remember, if your opponent doesn't know exactly where you are, he won't be able to effectively counterattack.

In many ways, your offensive skills must be comparable with a high-powered machine gun. During the course of your compound attack, it's imperative that you overwhelm your adversary by showering him with a barrage of rapid, successive blows designed to both injure him and demolish his defenses. Do you have the necessary firepower to neutralize your opponent?

Attack By Combination Demonstration #1

Step 1: From the neutral zone, Sammy Franco moves in with a quick push kick.

Step 2: Franco exploits his opponent's reaction dynamics with a rear uppercut punch.

Step 3: Franco immediately follows with a lead hook punch.

Step 4: Next, he follows with a rear hook.

Step 5: The opponent is finished off with a rear vertical knee to the face.

Breathing is one of the most important and often neglected aspects of fighting. Proper breathing promotes muscular relaxation and increases the speed and efficiency of your compound attack. The rate at which you breathe will also determine how quickly your body can recover from a violent encounter.

Attack By Combination Demonstration #2

Step 1: Franco initiates a finger jab strike to his opponent's eyes.

Step 2: He immediately follows up with a rear cross into his opponent's body.

Step 3: Next, is a lead horizontal elbow strike.

Step 4: Followed by a rear upper cut to the chin.

Step 5: The compound attack is finished with a rear hammer fist strike to the spine.

Learn to relax and avoid tensing your muscles when delivering a compound attack. Muscular tension will throw off your timing, retard the speed of your movements, and wear you out during a fight.

Attack By Combination Demonstration #3

Step 1: Franco is threatened at the punching range of unarmed combat. He immediately strikes first with a finger jab to his opponent's eyes.

Step 2: Franco sees the window of opportunity and attacks with a rear web hand strike to the opponent's throat.

Warning: the throat is considered a deadly force target and should only be struck in situations that legally warrant the application of lethal force.

Step 3: Franco exploits his opponent's reaction dynamics with a lead hook punch.

Step 4: Next, a powerful shovel hook to the solar plexus.

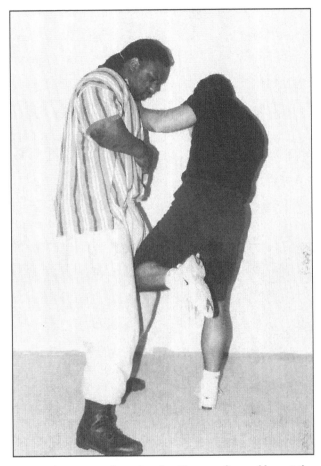

Step 5: The compound attack ends with a rear diagonal knee strike to the opponent's groin.

Always keep your chin angled slightly down when delivering a compound attack. This will make you a more elusive target and help minimize direct strikes to your eyes, nose, jaw, chin, and throat. However, avoid forcing your chin down too low. This will inhibit the mechanical fluidity of your tools and techniques and ultimately slow you down.

Attack by Combination Training

The Attack by Combination (ABC) method of attack can be developed in a variety of different ways. Here is a few suggestions that will get you started.

Heavy Bag Training

The heavy bag is tried-and-true for developing devastating compound attack techniques. It's no surprise that heavy bag work is regularly used in boxers, kick boxers, mixed martial artists, and self-defense practitioners. It's also popular among people who just want to stay in shape or add a new dimension to their fitness programs. Many people use the heavy bag for some of the following reasons:

- It conditions the entire body.

- It improves muscular endurance.

- It strengthens bones, tendons, and ligaments.

- It conditions the cardiovascular system.

- It relieves stress and helps channel aggressive energy.

The heavy bag is constructed of either top grain leather, canvas or vinyl. Most bags are 14 inches in diameter and 42 inches in length. The interior of the bag is filled with either cotton fiber, thick foam, sand or other durable material. Depending on the brand, heavy bags can weigh anywhere from seventy-five to two hundred and fifty pounds. However, for our purposes, I suggest a bag that weighs a minimum of 150 pounds.

Safe and effective heavy bag training will require you to find a place that will allow both you and the bag to move around freely. The location should also be a relatively quiet place that is free of distractions. Here are a few places you might want to consider:

- Garage

- Carport

- Basement

- Barn

- Home gym (if you are fortunate enough)

- Open field or backyard

- Warehouse

- Under a deck

Before you begin working out, invest in a good pair of bag gloves that will protect your hands when working out. When buying gloves, spare no expense and look for a reputable and high-quality brand. This will provide years of reliable use and will help ensure a better quality workout.

If you don't think you'll need bag gloves, think again. Striking the heavy bag without hand protection causes sore knuckles, bruised bones, hand inflammation, sore wrists and scraped knuckles. As a result, it will set your training back for several weeks in order for your hands to heal.

A good heavy bag workout consists of at least five rounds lasting three minutes in duration. Here are some important tips when working out on the bag:

1. Always warm up with some light stretching and calisthenics before working out.

2. Gradually build up the force of your blows. Remember, a beginner's wrists are too weak to accommodate full-force punches.

3. Never sacrifice balance for power.

4. Remember to snap your punches.

5. Always keep your wrists straight when striking the bag.

6. Always maintain proper form.

7. Move around and avoid remaining stationary.

8. Learn to integrate your kicks, punches, and strikes into logical compound attacks.

9. Pace yourself to avoid premature exhaustion.

10. Don't wear jewelry or a watch when training.

11. Stay relaxed and avoid unnecessary muscular tension.

12. Never hold your breath. Remember to exhale with the delivery of each and every technique.

13. Avoid the urge to stop the bag from moving. Let it swing freely!

14. If you don't know the proper way to throw a punch or kick, get instruction from a qualified coach or instructor.

15. Avoid heavy bag training two days in a row. Give your body a

few days to recover from your last workout.

Time-Based Heavy Bag Workouts

A time-based heavy bag workout is based on rounds, and it's an ideal way to structure your workouts. Before you begin, decide on the duration of your rounds as well as the rest intervals.

In most cases, mixed martial artists, boxers and kick boxers will work the heavy bag for three-minute rounds with one-minute rest periods. Depending on their level of conditioning and specific training goals, they might do this for a total of 5 to 10 rounds.

Initially, you'll need to experiment with both the round duration and rest intervals to see what works best for you. Remember to start off slow and progressively build up the intensity and length of your workouts. Don't forget to work with the bag and not try to kill it!

To get you started, here are some sample time-based workouts you might want to try. Keep in mind, the Advanced Level workouts are for elite fighters who have a minimum of 5 years of heavy bag training and conditioning.

Besides the actual body mechanics of punching, there are several other elements that comprise a punching combination. They include attack rhythms, height variations, the cadence of delivery, and practitioner movement.

Sample Time-Based Heavy Bag Workouts			
Skill Level	Duration of Each Round	Rest Period	Total Number of rounds
Beginner	1 minute	2 minutes	3
Beginner	1 minute	1 minute	3
Beginner	2 minutes	2 minutes	3
Beginner	2 minutes	1 minute	3
Intermediate	3 minutes	2 minutes	5
Intermediate	3 minutes	1 minute	5
Intermediate	3 minutes	2 minutes	6
Intermediate	3 minutes	1 minute	6
Advanced	4 minutes	2 minutes	8
Advanced	4 minutes	1 minute	8
Advanced	5 minutes	2 minutes	10
Advanced	5 minutes	1 minute	10

All time-based workouts will require you to invest in a workout timer. Luckily, there are dozens of smartphone apps that mimic the same features of an actual interval timer. These workout apps are convenient, inexpensive and can be found at your favorite online app store.

Focus Mitt Training

Focus mitt training is one of the best ways for developing and sharpening your compound attack skills. The focus mitt (also called punching mitt or focus pad) is an exceptional piece of training equipment that can be used by anyone. By placing the mitts at various angles and levels, you can perform every conceivable kick, punch, or strike known to mankind. Properly utilized, focus mitts will refine your defensive reaction time and condition your entire body for combat.

Focus mitts are constructed of durable leather designed to withstand tremendous punishment. Compared to other pieces of equipment, the focus mitt is relatively inexpensive. However, an effective workout requires two mitts (one for each hand). Your training partner (called the feeder) plays a vital role in focus mitt workouts by controlling the techniques you execute and the cadence of delivery. The intensity of your workouts will depend largely upon his or her ability to manipulate the mitts and push you to your limit. I often tell my students that a good focus mitt feeder is one step ahead of his training partner, whereas a great focus mitt feeder is two steps ahead of his partner.

When training with your partner, give them constructive feedback and let them know how he or she is doing. Remember, communication is vital during your workout sessions. Also, try to avoid remaining stationary. Get into the habit of constantly moving around with quick, economical steps.

To truly benefit from any focus mitt workout, you must learn to concentrate intensely throughout the entire session. You must block out both internal and external distractions. Try to visualize the focus mitt as a living, breathing assailant, not an inanimate target. This type of visualization will make the difference between a poor workout and a great training session. You also might want to draw small Xs on the mitts. This practice will improve your focus and concentration and help you develop accurate striking techniques.

Realistic street training drills can also be applied to the focus mitts. For example, if you applied the street training methodology you can prepare yourself for a ballistic street assault by having your training partner attack you with focus mitts from a variety of angles and ranges of combat. For twenty seconds, go after him with vicious and devastating strikes. Rest for one minute and then go again. The training possibilities are truly endless.

Never forget that offense is only half the game. Defensive skills are just as important and they must be practiced frequently to ensure that you will survive in the streets.

Full-Contact Sparring

Full-contact sparring is great for developing compound attack skills as well as self-confidence. It also develops many physical attributes like speed, quickness, coordination, agility, timing, distancing, ambidexterity, endurance, flexibility, tactile sensitivity, pain tolerance, finesse, accuracy, and non-telegraphic movement.

Once gain, sparring skills require combining kicks and punches into fluid and logical combinations. Basic sparring sessions are conducted at a moderate and controlled pace. The good news is you can spar just about anywhere, such as a gym, dojo, basement, garage and even outdoors. However, before you begin training, you'll need protective head gear, 14 oz boxing gloves, and a mouth piece.

Depending on your level of conditioning, sparring rounds can range anywhere from one to five minutes. Each round is separated by either 30-second, one-minute or two-minute breaks. A good sparring session consists of at least five to eight rounds.

Bruce Lee's 5 Methods of Attack

Since sparring workouts are structured around time, you will need a good workout timer. Most workout timers will allow you to adjust your round lengths anywhere from 30 seconds to 9 minutes. Rest periods can be changed from 30 seconds to 5 minutes depending on your level of conditioning and training goals.

When You Get Hit!

If and when you get hit in a sparring session, stay in control of your emotions and don't panic. Keep both hands up, stay mobile, and remain defensively alert. Maintain proper breathing, employ positive self-talk, and don't allow negative thoughts to contaminate your mind. Stay focused on the task at hand and continue to look for openings in your training partner's defenses.

Here are ten common mistakes that are made when sparring. Overcoming these errors will significantly enhance your mental toughness attributes.

1. Quitting or giving up after being hit.
2. Being distracted (internally or externally) when fighting.
3. Fearful or excessive blinking.
4. Randomly throwing punches or failing to focus on a particular target.
5. Lack of commitment when attacking your partner.
6. Hesitating or overthinking.
7. Turning your head away or closing your eyes when a blow is thrown at you.
8. Turning your body completely sideways from the sparring partner.
9. Running away from your opponent's attack.
10. Nervously swatting your sparring partner's boxing glove.

Shadowboxing or Shadow Fighting

Shadow fighting is the creative deployment of offensive and defensive techniques against imaginary assailants. It requires intense mental concentration, honest self-analysis, and a deep commitment to improving you fighting skills.

For someone on a tight budget, the good news is that shadow fighting is inexpensive. All you need is a full-length mirror and a place to work out. The mirror is vital. It functions as a critic, your personal instructor. If you're honest, the mirror will be too. It will point out every mistake - telegraphing, sloppy footwork, poor body mechanics, and even lack of physical conditioning.

Proper shadow fighting also develops speed, power, balance, footwork, compound attack skills, sound form, and finesse. It even promotes a better understanding of the ranges of combat. As you progress, you can incorporate light dumbbells or a weight vest into shadow fighting workouts to enhance power and speed.

A good shadow fighting workout consists of at least five rounds lasting three minutes in duration. Don't forget that you can also apply the proficiency and street training methodologies to your routine.

Fitness and Combat Conditioning

Finally, if you want to maximize the efficiency and effectiveness of the Attack by Combination method of attack, you must be physically fit. Fitness and conditioning comprises the following three broad components: cardiorespiratory conditioning, muscular/skeletal conditioning, and proper body composition.

The cardiorespiratory system includes the heart, lungs, and circulatory system, which undergo tremendous stress in a high-risk situation. So you're going to have to run, jog, bike, swim, or skip rope to develop sound cardiorespiratory conditioning. Each aerobic workout should last a minimum of 30 minutes and be performed at least four times per week.

The second component of conditioning is muscular/skeletal conditioning. To strengthen your bones and muscles to withstand the rigors of both sport and combat performance, your training must include progressive resistance (weight training). You will also need a stretching program designed to loosen up every muscle group. Stretching on a regular basis will also increase the muscles' range of motion, improve circulation, reduce the possibility of injury and relieve daily stress.

The final component of conditioning is proper body composition: simply, the ratio of fat to lean body tissue. Your diet and training regimen will affect your level or percentage of body fat significantly. A sensible and consistent exercise program accompanied by a healthy and balanced diet will facilitate proper body composition.

Bruce Lee's 5 Methods of Attack

Glossary

The following terms are defined in the context of Contemporary Fighting Arts and its related concepts. In many instances, the definitions bear little resemblance to those found in a standard dictionary.

A

accuracy—The precise or exact projection of force. Accuracy is also defined as the ability to execute a combative movement with precision and exactness.

adaptability—The ability to physically and psychologically adjust to new or different conditions or circumstances of combat.

advanced first-strike tools—Offensive techniques that are specifically used when confronted with multiple opponents.

aerobic exercise—Literally, "with air." Exercise that elevates the heart rate to a training level for a prolonged period of time, usually 30 minutes.

affective preparedness – One of the three components of preparedness. Affective preparedness means being emotionally, philosophically, and spiritually prepared for the strains of combat. See cognitive preparedness and psychomotor preparedness.

aggression—Hostile and injurious behavior directed toward a person.

aggressive response—One of the three possible counters when assaulted by a grab, choke, or hold from a standing position. Aggressive response requires you to counter the enemy with destructive blows and strikes. See moderate response and passive response.

aggressive hand positioning—Placement of hands so as to imply aggressive or hostile intentions.

agility—An attribute of combat. One's ability to move his or her body quickly and gracefully.

amalgamation—A scientific process of uniting or merging.

ambidextrous—The ability to perform with equal facility on both the right and left sides of the body.

anabolic steroids – synthetic chemical compounds that resemble the male sex hormone testosterone. This performance-enhancing drug is known to increase lean muscle mass, strength, and endurance.

analysis and integration—One of the five elements of CFA's mental component. This is the painstaking process of breaking down various elements, concepts, sciences, and disciplines into their atomic parts, and then methodically and strategically analyzing, experimenting, and drastically modifying the information so that it fulfills three combative requirements: efficiency, effectiveness, and safety. Only then is it finally integrated into the CFA system.

anatomical striking targets—The various anatomical body targets that can be struck and which are especially vulnerable to potential harm. They include: the eyes, temple, nose, chin, back of neck, front of neck, solar plexus, ribs, groin, thighs, knees, shins, and instep.

anchoring – The strategic process of trapping the assailant's neck or limb in order to control the range of engagement during razing.

assailant—A person who threatens or attacks another person.

assault—The threat or willful attempt to inflict injury upon the person of another.

assault and battery—The unlawful touching of another person without justification.

assessment—The process of rapidly gathering, analyzing, and accurately evaluating information in terms of threat and danger. You can assess people, places, actions, and objects.

attack—Offensive action designed to physically control, injure, or kill another person.

attack by combination (ABC) - One of the five methods of attack. See compound attack.

attack by drawing (ABD) - One of the five methods of attack. A method of attack predicated on counterattack.

attitude—One of the three factors that determine who wins a street fight. Attitude means being emotionally, philosophically, and spiritually liberated from societal and religious mores. See skills and knowledge.

attributes of combat—The physical, mental, and spiritual qualities that enhance combat skills and tactics.

awareness—Perception or knowledge of people, places, actions, and objects. (In CFA, there are three categories of tactical awareness: criminal awareness, situational awareness, and self-awareness.)

B

balance—One's ability to maintain equilibrium while stationary or moving.

blading the body—Strategically positioning your body at a 45-degree angle.

blitz and disengage—A style of sparring whereby a fighter moves into a range of combat, unleashes a strategic compound attack, and then quickly disengages to a safe distance. Of all sparring methodologies, the blitz and disengage most closely resembles a real street fight.

block—A defensive tool designed to intercept the assailant's attack by placing a non-vital target between the assailant's strike and your vital body target.

body composition—The ratio of fat to lean body tissue.

body language—Nonverbal communication through posture, gestures, and facial expressions.

body mechanics—Technically precise body movement during the execution of a body weapon, defensive technique, or other fighting maneuver.

body tackle – A tackle that occurs when your opponent haphazardly rushes forward and plows his body into yours.

body weapon—Also known as a tool, one of the various body parts that can be used to strike or otherwise injure or kill a criminal assailant.

burn out—A negative emotional state acquired by physically over- training. Some symptoms include: illness, boredom, anxiety, disinterest in training, and general sluggishness.

C

cadence—Coordinating tempo and rhythm to establish a timing pattern of movement.

cardiorespiratory conditioning—The component of physical fitness that deals with the heart, lungs, and circulatory system.

centerline—An imaginary vertical line that divides your body in half and which contains many of your vital anatomical targets.

choke holds—Holds that impair the flow of blood or oxygen to the brain.

circular movements—Movements that follow the direction of a curve.

close-quarter combat—One of the three ranges of knife and

bludgeon combat. At this distance, you can strike, slash, or stab your assailant with a variety of close-quarter techniques.

cognitive development—One of the five elements of CFA's mental component. The process of developing and enhancing your fighting skills through specific mental exercises and techniques. See analysis and integration, killer instinct, philosophy, and strategic/tactical development.

cognitive exercises—Various mental exercises used to enhance fighting skills and tactics.

cognitive preparedness – One of the three components of preparedness. Cognitive preparedness means being equipped with the strategic concepts, principles, and general knowledge of combat. See affective preparedness and psychomotor preparedness.

combat-oriented training—Training that is specifically related to the harsh realities of both armed and unarmed combat. See ritual-oriented training and sport-oriented training.

combative arts—The various arts of war. See martial arts.

combative attributes—See attributes of combat.

combative fitness—A state characterized by cardiorespiratory and muscular/skeletal conditioning, as well as proper body composition.

combative mentality—Also known as the killer instinct, this is a combative state of mind necessary for fighting. See killer instinct.

combat ranges—The various ranges of unarmed combat.

combative utility—The quality of condition of being combatively useful.

combination(s)—See compound attack.

common peroneal nerve—A pressure point area located approximately four to six inches above the knee on the midline of the outside of the thigh.

composure—A combative attribute. Composure is a quiet and focused mind-set that enables you to acquire your combative agenda.

compound attack—One of the five conventional methods of attack. Two or more body weapons launched in strategic succession whereby the fighter overwhelms his assailant with a flurry of full speed, full-force blows.

conditioning training—A CFA training methodology requiring the practitioner to deliver a variety of offensive and defensive combinations for a 4-minute period. See proficiency training and street training.

contact evasion—Physically moving or manipulating your body to avoid being tackled by the adversary.

Contemporary Fighting Arts—A modern martial art and self-defense system made up of three parts: physical, mental, and spiritual.

conventional ground-fighting tools—Specific ground-fighting techniques designed to control, restrain, and temporarily incapacitate your adversary. Some conventional ground fighting tactics include: submission holds, locks, certain choking techniques, and specific striking techniques.

coordination—A physical attribute characterized by the ability to perform a technique or movement with efficiency, balance, and accuracy.

counterattack—Offensive action made to counter an assailant's initial attack.

courage—A combative attribute. The state of mind and spirit that enables a fighter to face danger and vicissitudes with confidence, resolution, and bravery.

creatine monohydrate—A tasteless and odorless white powder that mimics some of the effects of anabolic steroids. Creatine is a safe body-building product that can benefit anyone who wants to increase their strength, endurance, and lean muscle mass.

criminal awareness—One of the three categories of CFA awareness. It involves a general understanding and knowledge of the nature and dynamics of a criminal's motivations, mentalities, methods, and capabilities to perpetrate violent crime. See situational awareness and self-awareness.

criminal justice—The study of criminal law and the procedures associated with its enforcement.

criminology—The scientific study of crime and criminals.

cross-stepping—The process of crossing one foot in front of or behind the other when moving.

crushing tactics—Nuclear grappling-range techniques designed to crush the assailant's anatomical targets.

D

deadly force—Weapons or techniques that may result in unconsciousness, permanent disfigurement, or death.

deception—A combative attribute. A stratagem whereby you delude your assailant.

decisiveness—A combative attribute. The ability to follow a tactical course of action that is unwavering and focused.

defense—The ability to strategically thwart an assailant's attack (armed or unarmed).

defensive flow—A progression of continuous defensive responses.

defensive mentality—A defensive mind-set.

defensive reaction time—The elapsed time between an assailant's physical attack and your defensive response to that attack. See offensive reaction time.

demeanor—A person's outward behavior. One of the essential factors to consider when assessing a threatening individual.

diet—A lifestyle of healthy eating.

disingenuous vocalization—The strategic and deceptive utilization of words to successfully launch a preemptive strike at your adversary.

distancing—The ability to quickly understand spatial relationships and how they relate to combat.

distractionary tactics—Various verbal and physical tactics designed to distract your adversary.

double-end bag—A small leather ball hung from the ceiling and anchored to the floor with bungee cord. It helps develop striking accuracy, speed, timing, eye-hand coordination, footwork and overall defensive skills.

double-leg takedown—A takedown that occurs when your opponent shoots for both of your legs to force you to the ground.

E

ectomorph—One of the three somatotypes. A body type characterized by a high degree of slenderness, angularity, and fragility. See endomorph and mesomorph.

effectiveness—One of the three criteria for a CFA body weapon, technique, tactic, or maneuver. It means the ability to produce a desired effect. See efficiency and safety.

efficiency—One of the three criteria for a CFA body weapon, technique, tactic, or maneuver. It means the ability to reach an objective quickly and economically. See effectiveness and safety.

emotionless—A combative attribute. Being temporarily devoid of human feeling.

endomorph—One of the three somatotypes. A body type characterized by a high degree of roundness, softness, and body fat. See ectomorph and mesomorph.

evasion—A defensive maneuver that allows you to strategically maneuver your body away from the assailant's strike.

evasive sidestepping—Evasive footwork where the practitioner moves to either the right or left side.

evasiveness—A combative attribute. The ability to avoid threat or danger.

excessive force—An amount of force that exceeds the need for a particular event and is unjustified in the eyes of the law.

experimentation—The painstaking process of testing a combative hypothesis or theory.

explosiveness—A combative attribute that is characterized by a sudden outburst of violent energy.

F

fear—A strong and unpleasant emotion caused by the anticipation or awareness of threat or danger. There are three stages of fear in order of intensity: fright, panic, and terror. See fright, panic, and terror.

feeder—A skilled technician who manipulates the focus mitts.

femoral nerve—A pressure point area located approximately 6 inches above the knee on the inside of the thigh.

fighting stance—Any one of the stances used in CFA's system. A strategic posture you can assume when face-to-face with an unarmed assailant(s). The fighting stance is generally used after you have launched your first-strike tool.

fight-or-flight syndrome—A response of the sympathetic nervous system to a fearful and threatening situation, during which it prepares your body to either fight or flee from the perceived danger.

finesse—A combative attribute. The ability to skillfully execute a movement or a series of movements with grace and refinement.

first strike—Proactive force used to interrupt the initial stages of an assault before it becomes a self-defense situation.

first-strike principle—A CFA principle that states that when physical danger is imminent and you have no other tactical option but to fight back, you should strike first, strike fast, and strike with authority and keep the pressure on.

first-strike stance—One of the stances used in CFA's system. A strategic posture used prior to initiating a first strike.

first-strike tools—Specific offensive tools designed to initiate a preemptive strike against your adversary.

fisted blows – Hand blows delivered with a clenched fist.

five tactical options – The five strategic responses you can make in a self-defense situation, listed in order of increasing level of resistance: comply, escape, de-escalate, assert, and fight back.

flexibility—The muscles' ability to move through maximum natural ranges. See muscular/skeletal conditioning.

focus mitts—Durable leather hand mitts used to develop and sharpen offensive and defensive skills.

footwork—Quick, economical steps performed on the balls of the feet while you are relaxed, alert, and balanced. Footwork is structured around four general movements: forward, backward, right, and left.

fractal tool—Offensive or defensive tools that can be used in more than one combat range.

fright—The first stage of fear; quick and sudden fear. See panic and terror.

full Beat – One of the four beat classifications in the Widow Maker Program. The full beat strike has a complete initiation and retraction phase.

G

going postal - a slang term referring to a person who suddenly and unexpectedly attacks you with an explosive and frenzied flurry of blows. Also known as postal attack.

grappling range—One of the three ranges of unarmed combat. Grappling range is the closest distance of unarmed combat from which you can employ a wide variety of close-quarter tools and techniques. The grappling range of unarmed combat is also divided into two planes: vertical (standing) and horizontal (ground fighting). See kicking range and punching range.

grappling-range tools—The various body tools and techniques that are employed in the grappling range of unarmed combat, including head butts; biting, tearing, clawing, crushing, and gouging tactics; foot stomps, horizontal, vertical, and diagonal elbow strikes, vertical and diagonal knee strikes, chokes, strangles, joint locks, and holds. See punching range tools and kicking range tools.

ground fighting—Also known as the horizontal grappling plane, this is fighting that takes place on the ground.

guard—Also known as the hand guard, this refers to a fighter's hand positioning.

guard position—Also known as leg guard or scissors hold, this is a ground-fighting position in which a fighter is on his back holding his opponent between his legs.

H

half beat – One of the four beat classifications in the Widow Maker Program. The half beat strike is delivered through the retraction phase of the proceeding strike.

hand immobilization attack (HIA) - One of the five methods of attack. A method of attack whereby the practitioner traps his opponent's limb or limbs in order to execute an offense attack of his own.

hand positioning—See guard.

hand wraps—Long strips of cotton that are wrapped around the hands and wrists for greater protection.

haymaker—A wild and telegraphed swing of the arms executed by an unskilled fighter.

head-hunter—A fighter who primarily attacks the head.

heavy bag—A large cylindrical bag used to develop kicking, punching, or striking power.

high-line kick—One of the two different classifications of a kick. A kick that is directed to targets above an assailant's waist level. See low-line kick.

hip fusing—A full-contact drill that teaches a fighter to "stand his ground" and overcome the fear of exchanging blows with a stronger opponent. This exercise is performed by connecting two fighters with a 3-foot chain, forcing them to fight in the punching range of unarmed combat.

histrionics—The field of theatrics or acting.

hook kick—A circular kick that can be delivered in both kicking and punching ranges.

hook punch—A circular punch that can be delivered in both the punching and grappling ranges.

I

impact power—Destructive force generated by mass and velocity.

impact training—A training exercise that develops pain tolerance.

incapacitate—To disable an assailant by rendering him unconscious or damaging his bones, joints, or organs.

initiative—Making the first offensive move in combat.

inside position—The area between the opponent's arms, where he has the greatest amount of control.

intent—One of the essential factors to consider when assessing a threatening individual. The assailant's purpose or motive. See demeanor, positioning, range, and weapon capability.

intuition—The innate ability to know or sense something without the use of rational thought.

J

jeet kune do (JKD) - "Way of the intercepting fist." Bruce Lee's approach to the martial arts, which includes his innovative concepts, theories, methodologies, and philosophies.

jersey Pull - Strategically pulling the assailant's shirt or jacket over his head as he disengages from the clinch position.

joint lock—A grappling-range technique that immobilizes the assailant's joint.

K

kick—A sudden, forceful strike with the foot.

kicking range—One of the three ranges of unarmed combat. Kicking range is the furthest distance of unarmed combat wherein you use your legs to strike an assailant. See grappling range and punching range.

kicking-range tools—The various body weapons employed in the kicking range of unarmed combat, including side kicks, push kicks, hook kicks, and vertical kicks.

killer instinct—A cold, primal mentality that surges to your consciousness and turns you into a vicious fighter.

kinesics—The study of nonlinguistic body movement communications. (For example, eye movement, shrugs, or facial gestures.)

kinesiology—The study of principles and mechanics of human movement.

kinesthetic perception—The ability to accurately feel your body during the execution of a particular movement.

knowledge—One of the three factors that determine who will win a street fight. Knowledge means knowing and understanding how to fight. See skills and attitude.

L

lead side -The side of the body that faces an assailant.

leg guard—See guard position.

linear movement—Movements that follow the path of a straight line.

low-maintenance tool—Offensive and defensive tools that require the least amount of training and practice to maintain proficiency. Low maintenance tools generally do not require preliminary stretching.

low-line kick—One of the two different classifications of a kick. A kick that is directed to targets below the assailant's waist level. (See high-line kick.)

lock—See joint lock.

M

maneuver—To manipulate into a strategically desired position.

MAP—An acronym that stands for moderate, aggressive, passive. MAP provides the practitioner with three possible responses to various grabs, chokes, and holds that occur from a standing position. See aggressive response, moderate response, and passive response.

martial arts—The "arts of war."

masking—The process of concealing your true feelings from your opponent by manipulating and managing your body language.

mechanics—(See body mechanics.)

mental attributes—The various cognitive qualities that enhance your fighting skills.

mental component—One of the three vital components of the CFA system. The mental component includes the cerebral aspects of fighting including the killer instinct, strategic and tactical development, analysis and integration, philosophy, and cognitive development. See physical component and spiritual component.

mesomorph—One of the three somatotypes. A body type classified by a high degree of muscularity and strength. The mesomorph possesses the ideal physique for unarmed combat. See ectomorph and endomorph.

mobility—A combative attribute. The ability to move your body quickly and freely while balanced. See footwork.

moderate response—One of the three possible counters when assaulted by a grab, choke, or hold from a standing position. Moderate response requires you to counter your opponent with a control and restraint (submission hold). See aggressive response and passive response.

modern martial art—A pragmatic combat art that has evolved to meet the demands and characteristics of the present time.

mounted position—A dominant ground-fighting position where a fighter straddles his opponent.

muscular endurance—The muscles' ability to perform the same motion or task repeatedly for a prolonged period of time.

muscular flexibility—The muscles' ability to move through maximum natural ranges.

muscular strength—The maximum force that can be exerted by a particular muscle or muscle group against resistance.

muscular/skeletal conditioning—An element of physical fitness that entails muscular strength, endurance, and flexibility.

N

naked choke—A throat choke executed from the chest to back position. This secure choke is executed with two hands and it can be performed while standing, kneeling, and ground fighting with the opponent.

neck crush – A powerful pain compliance technique used when the adversary buries his head in your chest to avoid being razed.

neutralize—See incapacitate.

neutral zone—The distance outside the kicking range at which neither the practitioner nor the assailant can touch the other.

nonaggressive physiology—Strategic body language used prior to initiating a first strike.

nontelegraphic movement—Body mechanics or movements that do not inform an assailant of your intentions.

nuclear ground-fighting tools—Specific grappling range tools designed to inflict immediate and irreversible damage. Nuclear tools and tactics include biting tactics, tearing tactics, crushing tactics, continuous choking tactics, gouging techniques, raking tactics, and all striking techniques.

O

offense—The armed and unarmed means and methods of attacking a criminal assailant.

offensive flow—Continuous offensive movements (kicks, blows, and strikes) with unbroken continuity that ultimately neutralize or terminate the opponent. See compound attack.

offensive reaction time—The elapsed time between target selection and target impaction.

one-mindedness—A state of deep concentration wherein you are free from all distractions (internal and external).

ostrich defense—One of the biggest mistakes one can make when defending against an opponent. This is when the practitioner looks away from that which he fears (punches, kicks, and strikes). His mentality is, "If I can't see it, it can't hurt me."

P

pain tolerance—Your ability to physically and psychologically withstand pain.

panic—The second stage of fear; overpowering fear. See fright and terror.

parry—A defensive technique: a quick, forceful slap that redirects an assailant's linear attack. There are two types of parries: horizontal and vertical.

passive response—One of the three possible counters when assaulted by a grab, choke, or hold from a standing position. Passive response requires you to nullify the assault without injuring your adversary. See aggressive response and moderate response.

patience—A combative attribute. The ability to endure and tolerate difficulty.

perception—Interpretation of vital information acquired from your senses when faced with a potentially threatening situation.

philosophical resolution—The act of analyzing and answering various questions concerning the use of violence in defense of yourself and others.

philosophy—One of the five aspects of CFA's mental component. A deep state of introspection whereby you methodically resolve critical questions concerning the use of force in defense of yourself or others.

physical attributes—The numerous physical qualities that enhance your combative skills and abilities.

physical component—One of the three vital components of the CFA system. The physical component includes the physical aspects of fighting, such as physical fitness, weapon/technique mastery, and combative attributes. See mental component and spiritual component.

physical conditioning—See combative fitness.

physical fitness—See combative fitness.

positional asphyxia—The arrangement, placement, or positioning of your opponent's body in such a way as to interrupt your breathing and cause unconsciousness or possibly death.

positioning—The spatial relationship of the assailant to the assailed person in terms of target exposure, escape, angle of attack, and various other strategic considerations.

postal attack - see going postal.

power—A physical attribute of armed and unarmed combat. The amount of force you can generate when striking an anatomical target.

power generators—Specific points on your body that generate impact power. There are three anatomical power generators: shoulders, hips, and feet.

precision—See accuracy.

preemptive strike—See first strike.

premise—An axiom, concept, rule, or any other valid reason to modify or go beyond that which has been established.

preparedness—A state of being ready for combat. There are three components of preparedness: affective preparedness, cognitive preparedness, and psychomotor preparedness.

probable reaction dynamics - The opponent's anticipated or predicted movements or actions during both armed and unarmed combat.

proficiency training—A CFA training methodology requiring the practitioner to execute a specific body weapon, technique, maneuver, or tactic over and over for a prescribed number of repetitions. See conditioning training and street training.

progressive indirect attack (PIA) – One of the five methods of attack. A progressive method of attack whereby the initial tool or technique is designed to set the opponent up for follow-up blows.

proxemics—The study of the nature and effect of man's personal space.

proximity—The ability to maintain a strategically safe distance from a threatening individual.

pseudospeciation—A combative attribute. The tendency to assign subhuman and inferior qualities to a threatening assailant.

psychological conditioning—The process of conditioning the mind for the horrors and rigors of real combat.

psychomotor preparedness—One of the three components of preparedness. Psychomotor preparedness means possessing all of the physical skills and attributes necessary to defeat a formidable adversary. See affective preparedness and cognitive preparedness.

punch—A quick, forceful strike of the fists.

punching range—One of the three ranges of unarmed combat. Punching range is the mid range of unarmed combat from which the fighter uses his hands to strike his assailant. See kicking range and grappling range.

punching-range tools—The various body weapons that are employed in the punching range of unarmed combat, including finger jabs, palm-heel strikes, rear cross, knife-hand strikes, horizontal and shovel hooks, uppercuts, and hammer-fist strikes. See grappling-range tools and kicking-range tools.

Q

qualities of combat—See attributes of combat.

quarter beat - One of the four beat classifications of the Widow Maker Program. Quarter beat strikes never break contact with the assailant's face. Quarter beat strikes are primarily responsible for creating the psychological panic and trauma when Razing.

R

range—The spatial relationship between a fighter and a threatening assailant.

range deficiency—The inability to effectively fight and defend in all ranges of combat (armed and unarmed).

range manipulation—A combative attribute. The strategic manipulation of combat ranges.

range proficiency—A combative attribute. The ability to effectively fight and defend in all ranges of combat (armed and unarmed).

ranges of engagement—See combat ranges.

ranges of unarmed combat—The three distances (kicking range, punching range, and grappling range) a fighter might physically engage with an assailant while involved in unarmed combat.

raze – To level, demolish or obliterate.

razer – One who performs the Razing methodology.

razing – The second phase of the Widow Maker Program. A series of vicious close quarter techniques designed to physically and psychologically extirpate a criminal attacker.

razing amplifier - a technique, tactic or procedure that magnifies the destructiveness of your razing technique.

reaction dynamics—see probable reaction dynamics.

reaction time—The elapsed time between a stimulus and the response to that particular stimulus. See offensive reaction time and defensive reaction time.

rear cross—A straight punch delivered from the rear hand that crosses from right to left (if in a left stance) or left to right (if in a right stance).

rear side—The side of the body furthest from the assailant. See lead side.

reasonable force—That degree of force which is not excessive for a particular event and which is appropriate in protecting yourself or others.

refinement—The strategic and methodical process of improving or perfecting.

relocation principle—Also known as relocating, this is a street-fighting tactic that requires you to immediately move to a new location (usually by flanking your adversary) after delivering a compound attack.

repetition—Performing a single movement, exercise, strike, or action continuously for a specific period.

research—A scientific investigation or inquiry.

rhythm—Movements characterized by the natural ebb and flow of related elements.

ritual-oriented training—Formalized training that is conducted without intrinsic purpose. See combat-oriented training and sport-oriented training.

S

safety—One of the three criteria for a CFA body weapon, technique, maneuver, or tactic. It means that the tool, technique, maneuver or tactic provides the least amount of danger and risk for the practitioner. See efficiency and effectiveness.

scissors hold—See guard position.

scorching – Quickly and inconspicuously applying oleoresin capsicum (hot pepper extract) on your fingertips and then razing your adversary.

self-awareness—One of the three categories of CFA awareness. Knowing and understanding yourself. This includes aspects of yourself which may provoke criminal violence and which will promote a proper and strong reaction to an attack. See criminal awareness and situational awareness.

self-confidence—Having trust and faith in yourself.

self-enlightenment—The state of knowing your capabilities, limitations, character traits, feelings, general attributes, and motivations. See self-awareness.

set—A term used to describe a grouping of repetitions.

shadow fighting—A CFA training exercise used to develop and refine your tools, techniques, and attributes of armed and unarmed combat.

sharking – A counter attack technique that is used when your adversary grabs your razing hand.

shielding wedge - a defensive maneuver used to counter an unarmed postal attack.

simple direct attack (SDA) – One of the five methods of attack. A method of attack whereby the practitioner delivers a solitary offenses tool or technique. It may involve a series of discrete probes or one swift, powerful strike aimed at terminating the encounter.

situational awareness—One of the three categories of CFA awareness. A state of being totally alert to your immediate surroundings, including people, places, objects, and actions. (See criminal awareness and self-awareness.)

skeletal alignment—The proper alignment or arrangement of your body. Skeletal alignment maximizes the structural integrity of striking tools.

skills—One of the three factors that determine who will win a street fight. Skills refers to psychomotor proficiency with the tools and techniques of combat. See Attitude and Knowledge.

slipping—A defensive maneuver that permits you to avoid an assailant's linear blow without stepping out of range. Slipping can be accomplished by quickly snapping the head and upper torso sideways (right or left) to avoid the blow.

snap back—A defensive maneuver that permits you to avoid an assailant's linear and circular blows without stepping out of range. The snap back can be accomplished by quickly snapping the head backward to avoid the assailant's blow.

somatotypes—A method of classifying human body types or builds into three different categories: endomorph, mesomorph, and ectomorph. See endomorph, mesomorph, and ectomorph.

sparring—A training exercise where two or more fighters fight each other while wearing protective equipment.

speed—A physical attribute of armed and unarmed combat. The rate or a measure of the rapid rate of motion.

spiritual component—One of the three vital components of the CFA system. The spiritual component includes the metaphysical issues and aspects of existence. See physical component and mental component.

sport-oriented training—Training that is geared for competition and governed by a set of rules. See combat-oriented training and ritual-oriented training.

sprawling—A grappling technique used to counter a double- or single-leg takedown.

square off—To be face-to-face with a hostile or threatening assailant who is about to attack you.

stance—One of the many strategic postures you assume prior to or during armed or unarmed combat.

stick fighting—Fighting that takes place with either one or two sticks.

strategic positioning—Tactically positioning yourself to either escape, move behind a barrier, or use a makeshift weapon.

strategic/tactical development—One of the five elements of CFA's mental component.

strategy—A carefully planned method of achieving your goal of engaging an assailant under advantageous conditions.

street fight—A spontaneous and violent confrontation between two or more individuals wherein no rules apply.

street fighter—An unorthodox combatant who has no formal training. His combative skills and tactics are usually developed in the street by the process of trial and error.

street training—A CFA training methodology requiring the practitioner to deliver explosive compound attacks for 10 to 20 seconds. See condition ng training and proficiency training.

strength training—The process of developing muscular strength through systematic application of progressive resistance.

striking art—A combat art that relies predominantly on striking techniques to neutralize or terminate a criminal attacker.

striking shield—A rectangular shield constructed of foam and vinyl used to develop power in your kicks, punches, and strikes.

striking tool—A natural body weapon that impacts with the assailant's anatomical target.

strong side—The strongest and most coordinated side of your body.

structure—A definite and organized pattern.

style—The distinct manner in which a fighter executes or performs his combat skills.

stylistic integration—The purposeful and scientific collection of tools and techniques from various disciplines, which are strategically integrated and dramatically altered to meet three essential criteria: efficiency, effectiveness, and combative safety.

submission holds—Also known as control and restraint techniques, many of these locks and holds create sufficient pain to cause the adversary to submit.

system—The unification of principles, philosophies, rules, strategies, methodologies, tools, and techniques of a particular method of combat.

T

tactic—The skill of using the available means to achieve an end.

target awareness—A combative attribute that encompasses five strategic principles: target orientation, target recognition, target selection, target impaction, and target exploitation.

target exploitation—A combative attribute. The strategic maximization of your assailant's reaction dynamics during a fight. Target exploitation can be applied in both armed and unarmed encounters.

target impaction—The successful striking of the appropriate anatomical target.

target orientation—A combative attribute. Having a workable knowledge of the assailant's anatomical targets.

target recognition—The ability to immediately recognize appropriate anatomical targets during an emergency self-defense situation.

target selection—The process of mentally selecting the appropriate anatomical target for your self-defense situation. This is predicated on certain factors, including proper force response, assailant's positioning, and range.

target stare—A form of telegraphing in which you stare at the anatomical target you intend to strike.

target zones—The three areas in which an assailant's anatomical targets are located. (See zone one, zone two and zone three.)

technique—A systematic procedure by which a task is accomplished.

telegraphic cognizance—A combative attribute. The ability to recognize both verbal and non-verbal signs of aggression or assault.

telegraphing—Unintentionally making your intentions known to your adversary.

tempo—The speed or rate at which you speak.

terminate—To kill.

terror—The third stage of fear; defined as overpowering fear. See fright and panic.

timing—A physical and mental attribute of armed and unarmed combat. Your ability to execute a movement at the optimum moment.

tone—The overall quality or character of your voice.

tool—See body weapon.

traditional martial arts—Any martial art that fails to evolve and change to meet the demands and characteristics of its present environment.

traditional style/system—See traditional martial arts.

training drills—The various exercises and drills aimed at perfecting combat skills, attributes, and tactics.

trap and tuck – A counter move technique used when the adversary attempts to raze you during your quarter beat assault.

U

unified mind—A mind free and clear of distractions and focused on the combative situation.

use of force response—A combative attribute. Selecting the appropriate level of force for a particular emergency self-defense situation.

V

viciousness—A combative attribute. The propensity to be extremely violent and destructive often characterized by intense savagery.

violence—The intentional utilization of physical force to coerce, injure, cripple, or kill.

visualization—Also known as mental visualization or mental imagery. The purposeful formation of mental images and scenarios in the mind's eye.

W

warm-up—A series of mild exercises, stretches, and movements designed to prepare you for more intense exercise.

weak side—The weaker and more uncoordinated side of your body.

weapon and technique mastery—A component of CFA's physical component. The kinesthetic and psychomotor development of a weapon or combative technique.

weapon capability—An assailant's ability to use and attack with a particular weapon.

webbing - The first phase of the Widow Maker Program. Webbing is a two hand strike delivered to the assailant's chin. It is called Webbing because your hands resemble a large web that wraps around the enemy's face.

widow maker – One who makes widows by destroying husbands.

widow maker program – A CFA combat program specifically designed to teach the law abiding citizen how to use extreme force when faced with immediate threat of unlawful deadly criminal attack. The Widow Maker program is divided into two phases or methodologies: Webbing and Razing.

Y

yell—A loud and aggressive scream or shout used for various strategic reasons.

Z

zero beat – One of the four beat classifications of the Widow Maker, Feral Fighting and Savage Street Fighting Programs. Zero beat strikes are full pressure techniques applied to a specific target until it completely ruptures. They include gouging, crushing, biting, and choking techniques.

zone one—Anatomical targets related to your senses, including the eyes, temple, nose, chin, and back of neck.

zone three—Anatomical targets related to your mobility, including thighs, knees, shins, and instep.

zone two—Anatomical targets related to your breathing, including front of neck, solar plexus, ribs, and groin.

Bruce Lee's 5 Methods of Attack

About Sammy Franco

With over 30 years of experience, Sammy Franco is one of the world's foremost authorities on armed and unarmed self-defense. Highly regarded as a leading innovator in combat sciences, Mr. Franco was one of the premier pioneers in the field of "reality-based" self-defense and martial arts instruction.

Sammy Franco is perhaps best known as the founder and creator of Contemporary Fighting Arts (CFA), a state-of-the-art offensive-based combat system that is specifically designed for real-world self-defense. CFA is a sophisticated and practical system of self-defense, designed specifically to provide efficient and effective methods to avoid, defuse, confront, and neutralize both armed and unarmed attackers.

Sammy Franco has frequently been featured in martial art magazines, newspapers, and appeared on numerous radio and television programs. Mr. Franco has also authored numerous books, magazine articles, and editorials, and has developed a popular library of instructional videos.

Sammy Franco's experience and credibility in the combat science is unequaled. One of his many accomplishments in this field includes the fact that he has earned the ranking of a Law Enforcement Master Instructor, and has designed, implemented, and taught officer survival training to the United States Border Patrol (USBP). He has instructed members of the US Secret Service, Military Special Forces,

Bruce Lee's 5 Methods of Attack

Washington DC Police Department, Montgomery County, Maryland Deputy Sheriffs, and the US Library of Congress Police. Sammy Franco is also a member of the prestigious International Law Enforcement Educators and Trainers Association (ILEETA) as well as the American Society of Law Enforcement Trainers (ASLET) and he is listed in the "Who's Who Director of Law Enforcement Instructors."

Sammy Franco is a nationally certified Law Enforcement Instructor in the following curricula: PR-24 Side-Handle Baton, Police Arrest and Control Procedures, Police Personal Weapons Tactics, Police Power Handcuffing Methods, Police Oleoresin Capsicum Aerosol Training (OCAT), Police Weapon Retention and Disarming Methods, Police Edged Weapon Countermeasures and "Use of Force" Assessment and Response Methods.

Mr. Franco holds a Bachelor of Arts degree in Criminal Justice from the University of Maryland. He is a regularly featured speaker at a number of professional conferences and conducts dynamic and enlightening seminars on numerous aspects of self-defense and combat training.

On a personal level, Sammy Franco is an animal lover, who will go to great lengths to assist and rescue animals. Throughout the years, he's rescued everything from turkey vultures to goats. However, his most treasured moments are always spent with his beloved German Shepherd dogs.

For more information about Mr. Franco and his unique Contemporary Fighting Arts system, you can visit his website at: **SammyFranco.com**

Other Books by Sammy Franco

THE WIDOW MAKER PROGRAM
Extreme Self-Defense for Deadly Force Situations
by Sammy Franco

The Widow Maker Program is a shocking and revolutionary fighting style designed to unleash extreme force when faced with the immediate threat of an unlawful deadly criminal attack. In this unique book, self-defense innovator Sammy Franco teaches you his brutal and unorthodox combat style that is virtually indefensible and utterly devastating. With over 250 photographs and detailed step-by-step instructions, The Widow Maker Program teaches you Franco's surreptitious Webbing and Razing techniques. When combined, these two fighting methods create an unstoppable force capable of destroying the toughest adversary. 8.5 x 5.5, paperback, photos, illus, 218 pages.

INVINCIBLE
Mental Toughness Techniques for
Peak Performance
by Sammy Franco

Invincible is a treasure trove of battle-tested techniques and strategies for improving mental toughness in all aspects of life. It teaches you how to unlock the true power of your mind and achieve success in sports, fitness, high-risk professions, self-defense, and other peak performance activities. However, you don't have to be an athlete or warrior to benefit from this unique mental toughness book. In fact, the mental skills featured in this indispensable program can be used by anyone who wants to reach their full potential in life. 8.5 x 5.5, paperback, photos, illus, 250 pages.

MAXIMUM DAMAGE
Hidden Secrets Behind Brutal
Fighting Combination
by Sammy Franco

Maximum Damage teaches you the quickest ways to beat your opponent in the street by exploiting his physical and psychological reactions in a fight. Learn how to stay two steps ahead of your adversary by knowing exactly how he will react to your strikes before they are delivered. In this unique book, reality based self-defense expert Sammy Franco reveals his unique Probable Reaction Dynamic (PRD) fighting method. Probable reaction dynamics are both a scientific and comprehensive offensive strategy based on the positional theory of combat. Regardless of your style of fighting, PRD training will help you overpower your opponent by seamlessly integrating your strikes into brutal fighting combinations that are fast, ferocious and final! 8.5 x 5.5, paperback, 240 photos, illustrations, 238 pages.

SAVAGE STREET FIGHTING
Tactical Savagery as a Last Resort
by Sammy Franco

In this revolutionary book, Sammy Franco reveals the science behind his most primal street fighting method. Savage Street Fighting is a brutal self-defense system specifically designed to teach the law-abiding citizen how to use "Tactical Savagery" when faced with the immediate threat of an unlawful deadly criminal attack. Savage Street Fighting is systematically engineered to protect you when there are no other self-defense options left! With over 300 photographs and detailed step-by-step instructions, Savage Street Fighting is a must-have book for anyone concerned about real world self-defense. Now is the time to learn how to unleash your inner beast! 8.5 x 5.5, paperback, 317 photos, illustrations, 232 pages.

FIRST STRIKE
End a Fight in Ten Seconds or Less!
by Sammy Franco

Learn how to stop any attack before it starts by mastering the art of the preemptive strike. First Strike gives you an easy-to-learn yet highly effective self-defense game plan for handling violent close-quarter combat encounters. First Strike will teach you instinctive, practical and realistic self-defense techniques that will drop any criminal attacker to the floor with one punishing blow. By reading this book and by practicing, you will learn the hard-hitting skills necessary to execute a punishing first strike and ultimately prevail in a self-defense situation. And that's what it is all about: winning in as little time as possible. 8.5 x 5.5, paperback, photos, illustrations, 202 pages.

WAR MACHINE
How to Transform Yourself Into A Vicious & Deadly Street Fighter
by Sammy Franco

War Machine is a book that will change you for the rest of your life! When followed accordingly, War Machine will forge your mind, body and spirit into iron. Once armed with the mental and physical attributes of the War Machine, you will become a strong and confident warrior that can handle just about anything that life may throw your way. In essence, War

Machine is a way of life. Powerful, intense, and hard. 11 x 8.5, paperback, photos, illustrations, 210 pages.

KUBOTAN POWER
Quick and Simple Steps to Mastering the Kubotan Keychain
by Sammy Franco

With over 290 photographs and step-by-step instructions, Kubotan Power is the authoritative resource for mastering this devastating self-defense weapon. In this one-of-a-kind book, world-renowned self-defense expert, Sammy Franco takes thirty years of real-world teaching experience and gives you quick, easy and practical kubotan techniques that can be used by civilians, law enforcement personnel, or military professionals. The Kubotan is an incredible self-defense weapon that has helped thousands of people effectively defend themselves. Men, women, law enforcement officers, military, and security professionals alike, appreciate this small and discreet self-defense tool. Unfortunately, however, very little has been written about the kubotan, leaving it shrouded in both mystery and ignorance. As a result, most people don't know how to unleash the full power of this unique personal defense weapon. 8.5 x 5.5, paperback, 290 photos, illustrations, 204 pages.

THE COMPLETE BODY OPPONENT BAG BOOK
by Sammy Franco

In this one-of-a-kind book, Sammy Franco teaches you the many hidden training features of the body opponent bag that will improve your fighting skills and boost your conditioning. With detailed photographs, step-by-step instructions, and dozens of unique workout routines, The Complete Body Opponent Bag Book is the authoritative resource for mastering this lifelike punching bag. The Complete Body Opponent Bag Book covers stances, punching, kicking, grappling techniques, mobility and footwork, targets, fighting ranges, training gear, time based workouts, punching and kicking combinations, weapons training, grappling drills, ground fighting, and dozens of workouts that will challenge you for years to come. 8.5 x 5.5, paperback, 139 photos, illustrations, 206 pages.

CONTEMPORARY FIGHTING ARTS, LLC
"Real World Self-Defense Since 1989"
www.SammyFranco.com

Made in the USA
Lexington, KY
16 October 2015